Twenty-Two Texas Women:
Strong, Tough, and Independent

By Michele Bennett and
Barbara Bennett

EAKIN PRESS ▼ＥＰ Fort Worth, Texas
www.EakinPress.com

Copyright © 1996
By Michelle Bennett & Barbara Bennett
Published By Eakin Press
An Imprint of Wild Horse Media Group
P.O. Box 331779
Fort Worth, Texas 76163
1-817-344-7036
www.EakinPress.com
ALL RIGHTS RESERVED
1 2 3 4 5 6 7 8 9
Paperback ISBN 978-1-57168-476-9
Hardback ISBN 978-1-57168-062-4
eBook ISBN 978-1-68179-240-8

Library of Congress Cataloging-in-Publication Data

Bennett, Michele, 1961–
    Twenty-two Texas women : strong, tough, and independent / by Michele
Bennett and Barbara Bennett.
       p.   cm.
    Includes bibliographical references (p.   ).
    Summary: Biographies of women who were the first or best in their fields
including business, aviation, and medicine when such professions were not
considered appropriate for women.
    ISBN 1-57168-062-4
    1. Women — Texas — Biography — Juvenile literature. 2. Texas — Biography —
Juvenile literature. [1. Women — Texas — Biography. 2. Texas — Biography.]
I. Bennett, Barbara, 1937–   . II. Title.
CT3260.B45   1996
920.72'09764--dc20   95-37373
                                      CIP
                                      AC

Contents

Introduction

Vast and majestic, Texas has always held a special allure. She beckoned Coronado to her sunlit mountains in his search for gold. Centuries unfolded as Spanish, French, German, and British adventurers came to Texas.

Staking a claim to Texas wasn't easy. The harsh, untamed land rebelled against civilization just as a wild mustang bucks against the pressure of its first saddle. Weather extremes, floods, and Indian raids were a constant challenge to early Texas settlers. But those hardy people thrived under the rugged conditions.

Adventurers saw unlimited possibilities in the untamed land. They saw fortunes awaiting those with the courage and determination to make it theirs. Their spirit set them apart as romantics and visionaries; this became the spirit of Texas.

Texas women — strong, tough, and independent — were a unique group. To keep their families alive, Texas women of all races had to work as hard as, if not harder than, their husbands. Early explorers noted that Indian women in Texas did most of the hard work. Pioneer women worked beside the men while homesteading in undeveloped territory. Those women forced into the role of slavery had a "can-do" attitude like that of other Texas women.

Even though many years have passed since slavery and pioneer times, outstanding Texas women continue to earn respect.

The women in this book embody the spirit of Texas. Like the pioneer women who tilled the land and the suffragists who pushed for the right to vote, the women in this book have the distinction of being the first or best in their fields.

They are women who ventured into business, aviation, and medicine when it wasn't a "woman's place." These women overcame life's hardships and opened doors of opportunity to claim their part of Texas. Their spirit continues to shine in the accomplishments of outstanding Texas women.

CHAPTER 1

They Led The Way

Octber haze cast a glow across the sliver of black — just a dash along the blue horizon.

"Land ho!" cried the lookout, and Portuguese sailors crowded the deck of the flagship.

In full sail, the *Santa Maria* surged forward, the Spanish Cross blood red upon her mainsail. Christopher Columbus sighted the land in his spyglass. As his voyage across uncharted waters ended, a new era of exploration began.

That voyage, ending October 12, 1492, in the Bahamas, could be credited to one woman: Queen Isabella of Spain.

When thirty-five-year-old Isabella married King Ferdinand, the kingdoms of Castile and Aragon were united into a strong empire. Isabella, who sat at state meetings and co-signed all documents, wielded power in that empire. She showed her power by supporting Columbus' dream when his own king, John II of Portugal, refused.

She had extended the Spanish empire to the New World.

In that New World, women would not hold the power that was owned by Queen Isabella. But in the land that would become Texas, a few began to lead the way for other women who would make a profound difference in their state.

1

ROSA MARIA HINOJOSA DE BALLI

Grants From a King

It was 1790 in the land that would someday become Texas. Thirty-two-year-old Rosa Maria Hinojosa de Balli was taking possession of her piece of that land. Her friends stood in the glare of the harsh sun to witness the ceremony of possession that Spanish law decreed.

Pushing a spade into the soil, Rosa broke loose a hard, black dirt clod. A stiff breeze whipped at her clothes and pulled strands of curls from her loose knot of hair.

She stooped, gathered the dirt, and tossed it, with cupfuls of water, toward the four corners of her land.

To the south was the river, hidden from view by thick palmettos and slender willows. In other directions the land stretched flat and arid. Long grass provided cover for an endless variety of wildlife that found protection under the round, thorny pads of the prickly pear. Their food was on the mesquite and ebony trees that grew like stunted dwarfs on the dry, windswept land.

It was on July 4, 1774, that Rosa's father and husband had posted notice for the Llano Grande grant in the office of the *alcalde* in Reynosa. When the grant became available in 1790, both men were dead, and, according to Spanish law, Rosa inherited the fifteen leagues of land.

Her father, Capt. Juan Jose de Hinojosa, was among Conde Jose de Escandon's group of aristocratic Spanish colonists. The first Hernandez home at Camargo was a *jacal,* or shack made of brush and adobe.

When Captain Hinojosa became chief justice of the area, the family moved to Reynosa. There Rosa attended the parish school until she was twelve. Then she began her lessons in running a household. One day she would manage her own household of servants. The servants would dye wool and cotton, twist it into thread, and weave it into cloth. They would also grind corn daily.

Rosa would learn to hand-dip candles and boil the bark of the huisache tree to make dyes for staining leather.

Her parents arranged her marriage to Capt. Jose Balli, whose family was also among the first Spanish colonists to the area along the Rio Grande.

As settlers who had been in the colony more than six years, the Hernandez and Balli families were given the largest and best tracts of land. Next choice went to those who had been there from two to five years. Residents of less than two years, *agregados,* were allotted only pasture land.

By the time land allotments were made in 1767, the cattle brought from Spain and bred with wild stock were large herds. It was on the broad delta lands along the river where the first American cowboys roped and branded their cattle. On their long, narrow ranches, stretching from the muddy banks of the Rio Grande, the Spanish *vaqueros* adapted their Old World ranching practices to the New World.

The ranching was so successful that Escandon requested more land for his colonists. The only land available by that time was the wild stretch of tangled brush north of the river. No Europeans had set foot there since Spanish explorers, after claiming it for the Spanish crown, had abandoned the wilderness.

Colonists north of the Rio Grande met with more hardships than they had experienced in the more settled areas to the south. It was into this wild, unsettled land along the river that the Native Americans would make their stand against the encroaching Europeans. The French and English were pushing them from their homes and hunting grounds in other areas. The Spanish colonists were moving up from Mexico to take over more and more land along the river they called the *Rio Bravo.* In an effort to hold their land, Lipans and Comanches made attacks against the colonists. In 1792, more Indian attacks were made against the Spanish settlers than ever before, and soldiers were sent to protect the ranchers.

In their home in Reynosa, Rosa and her sons were removed from the danger of Indian attacks. The hardship for them was money. Although the land was free, Rosa had the expense of government fees. Settlers were required to help pay for clearing roads between adjoining tracts and building a chapel where colonists could worship and Indians could be converted to Catholicism.

Rosa was proud of Nicolas, her oldest son, when he went to Spain to study for the priesthood. When he returned, she held a three-day fiesta at her La Feria ranch and threw *pesetas* to the crowd of ranch hands and friends celebrating his homecoming.

Padre Balli, referred to as "my son, the priest" by Rosa, helped her with the estate. They applied for a grant to the Brazos de Santiago on the north end of the crescent-shaped island just off the coast in the Gulf of Mexico. That island stands as a memorial to Rosa's son, and his statue now welcomes visitors to South Padre Island.

In 1794, Rosa applied for San Salvador del Tule, a seventy-two-league grant, in the name of her son Juan Jose, who was a captain in the militia. For Chico, a sergeant in the militia, Rosa bought Las Castanas tract from the original grantees of the Concepcion de Carricitos grant.

Rosa was realizing her dream of a Hinojosa-Balli empire. Her family held one-third of the region settled as Nuevo Santander by Conde Escandon and later to be known as the Lower Rio Grande Valley. Her ranches became landmarks, and deeds to other land referred to the property of Rosa Hinojosa. Most of the empire was held in her name until her death.

After Rosa's death in 1803, the Hinojosa-Balli empire was rocked by political unrest. Dissatisfied with Spanish rule, the Province of Santander developed strong allegiance to Mexico. Spanish Royal Army officers called the area a "hotbed of rebellion" and arrested Juan Jose on possible charges of plotting to overthrow Spanish rule.

Juan Jose died soon after his release. Chico died a short time later. The Padre Island grant, renewed after Mexico won its independence from Spain in 1821, was both a Spanish and Mexican land grant. On December 13, 1829, a relative performed the ritual of possession because even Padre Balli was dead by then.

In 1976, in recognition of her strength in building and holding together such an empire, Rosa Maria Hinojosa de Balli was named as one of the ten outstanding pioneer mothers of Texas.

ADINA DE ZAVALA AND CLARA DRISCOLL

Remembering the Alamo!

"Remember the Alamo!" These famous words rallied Gen. Sam Houston's troops to victory at the Battle of San Jacinto just six weeks after the bloody massacre of 189 Alamo defenders in March 1836. The same words became the rallying cry for Adina de Zavala and the Daughters of the Republic of Texas (DRT) when they learned that the shrine of Texas' independence, the Alamo, was headed for destruction in 1903.

De Zavala and the DRT realized that what General Santa Anna and his troops had not destroyed in the battle would soon be lost to commercial exploitation and neglect. The Alamo, established in 1718 by the Roman Catholic church as Mission San Antonio de Valero and later used as a fortress, was badly damaged during the Mexicans' thirteen-day siege in 1836.

For sixty-seven years following the siege, the Alamo served a number of purposes. It was used as quartermaster's depot in 1847 and as an armory for a Civil War militia company.

Writer Frederick Law Olmstead described the Alamo in 1854 after a visit to San Antonio: "The Alamo . . . is now within the town and, in extent, probably, a mere wreck of its former grandeur. It consists of a few irregular stuccoed buildings, huddled against the old church, in a large court surrounded by a rude wall."

In 1877 the Catholic church sold the long barrack and courtyard to businessman Honore Grenet. He leased the chapel for use as a warehouse. After Grenet's death in 1885, his estate sold the long barrack to Hugo & Schmeltzer, a wholesale company. In 1902 Adina de Zavala learned of the fate of the hallowed battleground.

De Zavala was the granddaughter of Lorenzo de Zavala, a Texas patriot who signed the Texas Declaration of Independence and served as vice-president during the new republic's interim government.

Adina had grown up with a reverence for her state's history,

ADINA DE ZAVALA left her mark on Texas, placing a record number of historical markers at state landmarks.
— Courtesy of University of Texas Institute of Texan Cultures

having lived with the legacy of her famous grandfather. As she matured, her own philosophy of historical preservation was formed. She believed it was not enough to read about historic events; she thought that existing battle sites and landmarks should be maintained.

It was this belief that led her to do something about the Alamo's plight. She began her cause by organizing a chapter of the DRT in San Antonio in 1889. Her family had moved to San Antonio from Galveston for her father's health. She worked as a teacher, devoting much of her spare time to historical work.

The De Zavala Chapter's first project was to place a monument on Ben Milam's grave on March 6, 1892. That day is now known as Texas Heroes Day.

De Zavala was serving as a member of the state executive committee of the DRT in 1902 when she proposed that the organization work toward securing the Alamo mission's other buildings. Her own DRT chapter was appointed custodian of the Alamo Chapel, which the state of Texas had purchased in 1883 for $20,000.

When she learned that an eastern hotel company had offered $75,000 for the former battle site, De Zavala sought financial backers. She found financial support in Clara Driscoll, who would help save the historic site from destruction.

Born at St. Mary's, Texas, in 1881, Driscoll was the daughter of wealthy cattleman Robert Driscoll, Sr. She, too, was the descendant of Texas revolutionaries. Both of her grandfathers fought in the war for Texas independence. She would later become a success in her own right as an author, playwright, businesswoman, and the state's Democratic committeewoman for nearly twenty years.

In 1903, upon returning from college in Europe, she offered to help preserve the Alamo battle site and joined the De Zavala Chapter of the DRT. She was twenty-two years old when she wrote checks totaling nearly $65,000 to buy the fortress grounds, earning the name "Savior of the Alamo."

In 1905, Driscoll turned over the property's title to the state of Texas, which in turn reimbursed her for the money she had spent on the property. The state named the DRT caretakers of the Alamo. Their duty would be to preserve the site and refurbish

CLARA DRISCOLL wrote checks to purchase the Alamo property, saving it from destruction. Later reimbursed by the state, she would be known as the "Savior of the Alamo."

— Courtesy of University of Texas Institute of Texan Cultures

it as they saw fit. The state offered no guidelines to tell the group what should be spared, and the state offered no funds for repair work.

That's when the conflict, later termed "the Second Battle of the Alamo," began. According to historian Robert Ables' article for the January 1967 issue of *Southwestern Historical Quarterly,* there were two distinct views on the best way to present the Alamo fortress' history. The disagreement divided the DRT and caused a public uproar that was covered by newspapers and argued in several court cases. The argument was between those DRT members who wanted to focus on the Alamo Chapel and those who wanted to rebuild the long barracks to house a museum.

Driscoll sided with those who wanted to emphasize the chapel and build a park around the shrine. De Zavala was more of a historical purist. She sided with the group who favored restoring the long barracks, where the bloodiest fighting of the battle occurred.

For a year, the opposing factions debated the choices. By 1906, the Driscollites, as the chapel devotees were called, formed a new DRT chapter known as the Alamo Mission Chapter of San Antonio.

Five years after the squabble started, the DRT's state organization intervened and passed custodianship of the Alamo to the Alamo Mission Chapter. De Zavala's original DRT chapter was disaffiliated by the state organization and disbanded.

When renovations were completed, the chapel had been refurbished and one of the fortress walls remained standing. However, the convent (long barracks) wasn't restored until 1968, when it was converted into a museum.

De Zavala and Driscoll survived the "second battle of the Alamo," and both went on to contribute generously in their own ways.

De Zavala's desire was to maintain artifacts for future generations. She continued her preservation work by organizing and joining over thirty historical organizations throughout her long life. She founded the Texas Historical and Landmark Society, a group that placed historical markers throughout San Antonio. She was named to several state historical committees, including the governor's appointment to the Texas Historical Board in 1923.

De Zavala died in San Antonio at the age of ninety-four.

Driscoll married Henry Sevier in 1906 and traveled to South America with him when he was appointed ambassador to Chile. The two divorced in 1937.

Driscoll's accomplishments included writing two books about Texas. *The Girl of La Gloria* was a love story set in Texas. *In the Shadow of the Alamo* was a collection of Texan and Mexican legends of the Alamo.

Her philanthropic work included giving $92,000 to the State Federation of Women's Clubs to clear their debt. She also oversaw the charity programs of her family's Driscoll Foundation Children's Hospital.

When she died in 1945, her body lay in state in the Alamo Chapel.

De Zavala and Driscoll share a place in the annals of Texas. Their efforts left a piece of history standing for all to see so that no one will forget the bloody siege. De Zavala and Driscoll were there to remember the Alamo.

Chapter 2

They Served as First Ladies

Have you heard the joke about the president who met his wife's former boyfriend?

"Aren't you glad you married me?" he asked his wife later.

"Why?"

"If you'd married him, you wouldn't be married to a president."

"Oh, yes I would," she replied.

Behind every successful man, the saying goes, is a strong woman.

As a republic, Texas had the distinction of having presidents and presidential first ladies. One of them was Margaret Lea Houston, wife of Sam Houston. Called "Conqueress of the Conqueror," the twenty-three-year-old Margaret married forty-six-year-old Sam Houston in 1840. He met the girl from Alabama after he had fought in the War of 1812, represented Tennessee in the United States House of Representatives, been governor of Tennessee, divorced a wife in Tennessee, traded with the Indians, abandoned his Indian wife, commanded the Texian Army, and been elected president of the new Republic of Texas.

Margaret had persuaded the rugged frontiersman to drink less and join a church, but she couldn't persuade him to give up politics. He served in the Texas Congress and a second term as president after they married.

After Texas joined the United States, Margaret stayed in Texas while Sam represented the new state of Texas in the United States Senate. After he became governor she gave birth to their eighth child, Temple Lea Houston, the first child born in the Governor's Mansion in Austin.

Like later first ladies of presidents, of the United States, that is, Margaret followed her husband in his career and endured public scrutiny.

LADY BIRD JOHNSON

She Brought Beauty to Texas

It was the spring of hope, with wildflowers blooming along highways where junkyards once grew. It was the winter of despair, with young Americans dying in the jungles of Vietnam and on freedom buses at home.

It was the time of Lady Bird Johnson, and her life was as much of a contrast as those times.

Claudia Alta Taylor, born December 22, 1912, in Karnack, Texas, was nicknamed "Lady Bird" by a nursemaid who said that she was as "purty as a lady bird." Her mother died by the time Lady Bird was five, and her brothers were sent to boarding school.

Alone with her father, Lady Bird found entertainment in books. She read more books before she entered high school than most people read in a lifetime. She roamed the East Texas woods where a panorama of beauty unfolded year round. Lady Bird was often the only student in the one-room school attended by the sharecroppers who farmed her father's land.

Self-sufficient and independent, Lady Bird often planned and organized activities with her friends. They knew that it would take a forceful man to win Lady Bird's heart.

*LADY BIRD JOHNSON made beautification a priority
during her years as first lady.*
— Courtesy of Lady Bird Johnson

13

That forceful man was Lyndon Baines Johnson. When she met him in September of 1934, she said that she was attracted to the charismatic young politician "like a moth drawn to a flame." They eloped and were married in St. Mark's Episcopal Church in San Antonio on November 17, 1934. The couple lived in a small apartment in Washington, D.C., where Lyndon worked in Congressman Richard Kleberg's office.

The difference between Lady Bird and Lyndon was the difference between the closed-in East Texas pine thicket and the wide-open, rolling Hill Country. It was also the difference between wealth and poverty. Lady Bird's father, Thomas Jefferson Taylor, was a successful businessman who worked long hours at amassing a fortune. Sam Johnson farmed, ranched, and sold real estate when he wasn't campaigning for and working in the state legislature. However, his hard work did not result in a fortune.

With a bank account and car at her disposal, Lady Bird led a secure life. But the threat of foreclosure hung over Lyndon's youth like storm clouds over a Texas hillside in the spring.

The Johnson children carried on spirited debates tutored by their father. Lyndon was told, "You better eyeball the person you are speaking to and know what you are saying." Lady Bird, who quietly pursued her own interests, was as shy about speaking as Lyndon was bold. When she graduated from Marshall High School in May of 1928, fifteen-year-old Lady Bird breathed a sigh of relief that her class ranking was number three. Only the top two students had to give a commencement address.

Lady Bird summed up their differences by saying, "He made me try harder and do more. I made him take a gentler attitude and be less impatient." Despite their differences, Lady Bird and Lyndon were alike in their desire to be somebody of importance.

Lyndon liked to entertain those who could promote his political career. Lady Bird planned menus, decorated the table, and cooked meals — things servants had done for her before her marriage. She always saw to her guests' comfort, even though she felt shy and nervous herself.

She overcame some of her shyness when she took over the management of her husband's congressional office while he served in the navy during World War II. She became confident after running his office, and felt that if it was ever necessary she could make her own living.

She liked the feeling of being a businesswoman so much that she decided to go into business. Using money from her mother's estate, Lady Bird bought a radio station in Austin. She studied the financial books of the failing station and worked to make it a profitable business.

She had become a successful businesswoman and had bought a home in Washington. She was disappointed that she did not have children after ten years of marriage and three miscarriages. Then Lynda Bird was born, on March 19, 1944. After another miscarriage, Lucy Baines was born, on July 2, 1947.

When Lyndon ran for vice-president on the Democratic ticket with John F. Kennedy in 1960, Lady Bird became the first woman to campaign in a presidential election. During the campaign she traveled 35,000 miles in seventy-one days, made sixteen solo appearances in eleven states, made 150 appearances with her husband, gave sixty-five "greeting" talks from the campaign train, and attended receptions with Kennedy's sisters.

In a speech to young people she once said, "Do something out of character. It proves you're alive." During her years as wife of the vice-president, she followed that advice. She saw thirty-three foreign countries in 120,000 miles of travel. She represented the United States as goodwill ambassador around the world.

After two years and ten months as second lady, she was prepared to move into the White House as first lady. She did that after President Kennedy's assassination on November 22, 1963. Lady Bird had flown into Dallas that day in the dazzle of sunlight and felt pride at her home state's rousing welcome. That pride had turned to grief at the turn of a corner on Sixth Street. The flight out of Dallas on that dark November night was as somber as the casket aboard.

As first lady, Lady Bird sought ways to improve women's lives. She traveled to poor regions of the United States to check on the progress of Johnson's Great Society. As she traveled, she saw industrial squalor on the outskirts of most towns. The mess offended the naturalist who had spent most of her life enjoying the rural beauty of East Texas. It even appalled her. As a woman who had traveled worldwide, she knew that roadsides provided a traveler's first impression. The beauty of the land became her concern, and highway beautification became her project.

But no amount of beautification could cover up the fact that great injustices were being committed against American citizens at home and in Vietnam. Civil rights bills had to be enforced, not just passed. Troops had to be backed, not just sent. There were many difficult issues to face during those times.

After leaving the White House in 1968, Lady Bird served on the board of regents for the University of Texas for six years. She considered it "the biggest thing that ever happened to me on my own."

Lady Bird also continued her beautification efforts by seeing to it that places along the highway were cleaned up and that wild-flowers were planted wherever possible. In 1982 she gave $125,000 and sixty acres of land to establish the National Wild-flower Research Center in Austin. Lady Bird said that the center is "an effort to fill a little niche in the whole environmental picture." Her beautification efforts, still a contrast to harsh reality, adorn Texas highways every spring.

BARBARA BUSH

A Legacy of Literacy

According to Democrat Ann Richards in a keynote address, Republican George Bush was born with a "silver foot" in his mouth. But the woman at his side is pure gold.

Barbara Pierce was born on June 8, 1925, and grew up in Rye, New York. Barbara was sixteen and attending Ashley Hall School in Charleston, South Carolina, in 1942, when she met George Wallace Bush at a Christmas dance in Greenwich, Connecticut. She was attracted to the handsome, young man, who, at eighteen, was one of the youngest pilots in the navy.

George recognized the pretty girl with the twinkling eyes as someone special. They corresponded after George went overseas and Barbara entered Smith College in North Hampton, Massachusetts.

Former first lady BARBARA BUSH continues to fight illiteracy.
— Courtesy of Barbara Bush

In September of 1944, George's plane was hit. One crewman was killed, but George piloted the disabled plane over the target to complete his bombing mission. As George bailed out of the flaming plane, he cut his head. Landing in the ocean, he drifted for several hours and watched the horizon for approaching craft. Would it be ally or enemy? Would he ever see Barbara again?

The happy ending was that an American submarine rescued him, President Franklin Roosevelt awarded him the Distinguished Flying Cross, and Barbara married him on January 6, 1945.

Barbara had planned to become a nurse but decided to become a full-time wife. "In the 1940s American women did not expect to have careers of their own," she said.

George was in the service during the first eight months of their marriage and attended Yale University after his discharge. After graduation, he worked in Odessa, Texas, where they lived in a bright-colored house that Barbara called her Easter egg house. George, Jr., had been born by then, and Pauline (Robin) was born the year after they moved to Texas.

By 1950, when they moved to Midland, Texas, their daughter Robin was diagnosed with leukemia and died in 1953. Depression whirled in Barbara's mind like the sand storms that whipped around her Midland home. One day, as she sat, wrapped in her despair, she overheard her son telling his friend, "I have to play with my mother. She's sad."

That was the jolt that Barbara needed to jump start her life again. And jump is what Barbara had to do as her family grew. John Ellis (JEB) was born in 1953. Soon after the birth of Neil in 1955, the Bushes moved to Houston. Even with three small sons, Barbara found time to help others. She started the "next-to-new" shop to redistribute donated clothing. In memory of her daughter Robin, Barbara began fund-raising for leukemia research. She was named national honorary chairperson of the Leukemia Society.

The births of Marvin and Dorothy completed the Bush family. The Bushes gave their children large doses of love and taught them to be honest and to do their best.

The family lived in Washington for four years when George served in the House of Representatives. They lived in New York when he was ambassador to the United Nations, and in China when he served as a United States envoy to the People's Republic of China. In 1981 the Bush family moved into the Vice-President's Mansion.

When she became second lady, Barbara began to work on the project of promoting literacy. Barbara always considered reading a great satisfaction and an essential skill that can't be taken for granted. Her campaign to fight illiteracy included increasing public awareness of the literacy problem, persuading groups and individuals to work toward solving the problem, and speaking in behalf of successful efforts.

Barbara appeared on a TV special to celebrate the bicentennial of the Constitution and to promote literacy. The highlight of the program was when Barbara read the preamble of the Constitution with J. T. Pace, a retired construction worker who had learned to read through the literacy training program. As Barbara and J. T. embraced, the audience rose in a standing ovation.

Barbara recommends reading aloud to help children develop an interest in reading. She reads at libraries during story time. "Mrs. Bush's Story Time" is a national radio program emphasizing the importance of reading aloud to children. She feels that adult literacy breaks the cycle of illiteracy. As honorary chairman of the Barbara Bush Foundation for Family Literacy, she hopes to establish literacy as a value in every American family.

When Barbara visits literacy classes, she hears adults tell how learning to read has given them the chance to get a better job. She has been told by prisoners that being able to read is like being set free from prison.

Barbara is the author of several books. *C. Fred's Story* tells about the life of the vice-president's family as seen by their dog, C. Fred. *Millie's Book* is about another dog's life in the White House. Millie was thrilled when so many visitors asked to see her that she was called downstairs to meet them. The gardens around the White House were Millie's favorite spot. A special garden that Lady Bird Johnson made for the children and grandchildren of presidents provided a quiet spot to meditate. Another private garden near the Oval Office was where Millie could watch a game of horseshoes almost every day.

Proceeds from both books are donated to adult and family literacy programs.

After leaving the White House in 1993, Barbara wrote *A Memoir, Barbara Bush.* It reviews all of the interesting things she has done. Barbara wrote, "I had the best job in America. Every single day was interesting, rewarding, and sometimes just plain fun." She enjoyed "meeting, seeing, hearing, and enjoying the best of the best our country has to offer."

Every spring, Barbara received more than a hundred invitations to give commencement addresses. In 1990, she accepted an invitation to speak at the graduation ceremonies at Wellesley College in Massachusetts. A few of the students at the all-girl school protested that Barbara Bush did not represent the Wellesley image of women who gain recognition on their own, not on their husband's achievements. Barbara told the graduates that women don't have to be married and have children, but if they have children, those children must come first.

Barbara said that she had many opportunities to continue her college education and pursue a career, but she has never regretted staying home to care for her large family.

Since leaving the White House, Barbara has continued her fight against illiteracy while enjoying retirement from public life. As her husband said, "Life is absolutely wonderful." True words from a man who recognized gold when he saw it.

Chapter 3

They Entered the
Business World

Woman's place was in the home. On the prairie it was a full-time job of plowing, planting, harvesting, spinning, weaving, sewing, candle-making, bread-making, child-bearing.

The industrial revolution moved jobs from the home to factories. Cultural revolutions moved women out into the work places and the stores. But even then, women saw a division of roles and kept to their place as secretaries or assembly line workers. Women very rarely owned a business. Married women couldn't own businesses because their husbands did that. Widows were often the only women who could afford to own a business. If there was no family business for a widow to "take-over," she sometimes had to start her own. The family home became a boardinghouse, a laundry, or a seamstress' shop. Some plucky Texas women ran ranches or farms after their husbands died.

Over the years, wars left women in charge of business at home while their husbands went off to the battlefield. During World War II, women referred to as "Rosie the Riveter" built war planes and ammunition. Women Air Service Pilots, or WASPs, helped train fighter pilots in those planes at Edinburg and Sweetwater.

After the war, Rosie didn't want to be stuck in the kitchen again — especially since American technology had turned from producing war machines to producing household gadgets. Modern appliances, shiny automobiles, and prepared foods lured women into the job market.

Striving toward equal rights in the business world, women often formed their own companies. They had learned from their brothers that was the way to success.

Based on traits they possessed as leaders, skills they acquired in the work place, and persistence they owned as survivors, many Texas women stand out as examples of business success.

FLORENCE BUTT

A Country Store

Walking through the door of the tiny Kerrville grocery store, you wonder where the bakery is. And you need to fill your allergy prescription, so where's the pharmacy? This is an HEB store, isn't it? "This is the C. C. Butt Staple and Fancy Groceries," says a kindly clerk. "We can help you find what you need. You're welcome to charge your groceries, and my boys will deliver them if you like."

"Credit? Cool!" As you look around the store you notice wooden crates full of apples and potatoes. You scan narrow shelves lined with neat rows of canned goods. "Defender Tomatoes? I've never heard of that brand."

The unmistakable smell of pickles draws you toward a barrel full of them. Then your gaze falls on a calendar: April 1906.

This isn't any ordinary HEB store. It's the very first store. The clerk isn't just an employee, either. She's Florence Butt, founder of the Texas grocery giant, HEB.

This would be your experience if you could travel back in time. You'd see the humble beginnings of what is today the largest privately owned grocery in the nation — HEB.

Today's HEB Superstores are a model of convenience for grocery shoppers. You can eat a sandwich in the deli while you wait for your film to develop at the photo processing center, buy

HEB founder FLORENCE BUTT and family. Howard is on her right.
— Courtesy of HEB Archives

your groceries, pay your phone bill, and pick up a video all in the same building.

Size and versatility aside, today's HEB organization shares in the same principles and beliefs that Florence held when she opened her credit and delivery store in the Texas Hill Country at the turn of the century. She stressed good service, cleanliness, and quality products at low prices.

Florence Thornton was born on September 19, 1864, in Buena Vista, Mississippi. Like many Southern women, she developed a strength of character that later helped her face family hardships and deaths. The fact that she was smart, hard-working, resourceful, determined, and devout in her religious beliefs helped Florence too.

She attended college while most women of her day were content to marry and start a family before they were twenty. At Clinton College in Mississippi, she was the only girl in class. She adjusted well and graduated in 1886 with a teaching degree. She taught in a rural school for three years until she met a pharmacist named Charles C. Butt. The two were married on February 11, 1889, and moved to Memphis, Tennessee.

Florence assumed the role of mother to widower Butt's two sons. The family grew with the birth of Florence and C.C.'s three sons, Charles, Jr., Eugene, and Howard.

Soon after Howard's birth, Charles, Sr., was diagnosed with tuberculosis. Doctors recommended the Texas Hill Country because of its climate and the availability of qualified medical help. Florence made the courageous decision to move her family thousands of miles to a small town where she had no family, friends, or job prospects.

Arriving in Kerrville in the early 1900s, Florence tried sales to support her family. She sold door-to-door for the A&P Tea Company.

Being a salesman went against Florence's dignified nature. Her son, Eugene, recalled years later that his mother's feelings were hurt when a prospective customer said, "I don't buy from peddlers," and slammed the door.

By 1905, Florence had saved $60 and used it to open her own grocery store on the ground floor of a two-story building she rented for nine dollars a month. The family lived above the store.

Florence christened her store "Mr. C. C. Butt Staple and Fancy Groceries" and held the grand opening November 26, 1905.

Grocery stores delivered in those days, so Florence enlisted the help of her three sons, who were fourteen, twelve, and ten years old by then. They pulled a converted baby carriage loaded with groceries. Later they bought a more respectable red toy wagon. Eventually, the Butts were able to afford a horse and wagon to use for deliveries. It was a family-run operation for the first few years until they hired their first employee in 1913 to help with increased business.

Her youngest son, Howard, showed a keen business sense. By the time he was fifteen years old, he had taken over many of the managerial duties. In the company's history Eugene told about Howard's industriousness. He said, "One thing (Howard) did was cause Mother to stock tobacco. She was opposed to this, but it was causing loss of trade." Florence's strong Christian faith influenced her decision not to sell liquor either. Howard agreed with her on this point, refusing to sell beer or wine in HEB stores until the late 1970s, when his staff convinced him that not stocking liquor would cause shoppers to go to rival stores.

Howard took over the family's Kerrville store in 1919. Florence, at age fifty-five, was ready to lighten her workload. She continued to work in the store for several more years. She welcomed customers, worked in the office, and made sandwiches in the delicatessen.

Howard made changes and took risks to expand the business. Converting to a cash-and-carry store was a gamble since credit was still the common business practice.

Expansion stores in Center Point, Junction, and Brownwood failed. Seven years later, in 1926, an expansion store in Del Rio was a success.

With a second store and a new company name, the C. C. Butt Cash and Carry was off to a good start. Two years later, Howard borrowed $38,000 to buy three bankrupt Piggly Wiggly stores in the Rio Grande Valley. He saw opportunity in the southernmost area of Texas.

In 1928 Howard moved company headquarters to Brownsville to be closer to his new territory. The company flourished after the move. Maybe that was due to Howard's ability to give the customers what they wanted.

He built customer loyalty by maintaining a price cap on staples like flour and sugar. As the company grew, Howard opened bakeries, canneries, and a dairy plant to supply his store, keeping retail prices low by eliminating a middle man.

Howard also had a flair for creative marketing. He and store managers tossed nickels off store roofs at grand openings. They attached tags for free groceries to the legs of live chickens and set them free in store parking lots.

He revolutionized the grocery business by departmentalizing his stores in the 1930s. In 1949 in Corpus Christi he opened his first "super store" with a pharmacy, cosmetics department, and lunch counter.

In 1935 Florence Butt officially handed the title of chief executive officer to forty-year-old Howard. He changed the business name to H. E. Butt Grocery Company. The chain had twenty-eight stores by the mid-1930s. Howard's vision was to open one hundred stores throughout Texas.

Howard never forgot the lessons of charity he learned from his mother. Every Christmas, Florence and her sons left baskets on the porches of needy families on Christmas morning. As the Butts' success grew, so did the charity work. In 1933, Howard formed the H. E. Butt Foundation to fund medical, educational, and recreational programs in the South Texas communities HEB served. Programs sponsored by the company's foundation have included a tennis complex in Corpus Christi, a youth camp near Leakey, Texas, libraries, swimming pools, and tennis courts in several Texas communities.

The company assists during emergencies. In the past they have sent food to hurricane victims in Louisiana and North Carolina and to earthquake survivors in Mexico.

On March 4, 1954, HEB's founder died at her home in Kerrville. The store Florence started with $60 and a prayer has grown into the largest privately owned food chain in the nation, with approximately 225 stores in 120 towns and cities.

Mary Kay Ash

Looking Good With Class

Texas farm wives were not noted for their interest in cosmetics. Standing over a steaming pot while preparing dinner was the closest most of them got to a facial. Back when dressing for company meant turning an apron clean side out, make-up consisted of a swipe of lipstick and a pat of powder purchased at the "dime store."

Eventually, something happened to change that. Friends began inviting friends to gather around the kitchen table to clean, condition, and cosmetically enhance their faces. Neighbors were invited to become dealers in beauty themselves. While helping their friends to a better complexion, the beauty dealers helped themselves to a better life. A life of furs, jewelry, and Cadillacs! Pink Cadillacs! They had one person to thank for it all: a tiny Texas woman named Mary Kay.

Mary Kay Ash learned self-confidence and competence at a young age. When she was seven years old, Ash took care of her invalid father while her mother worked long hours as a restaurant manager.

"You can do it," was the encouragement Ash's mother gave her. Ash learned to cook and clean and went downtown alone on the bus to buy her own clothes.

Responsibility at an early age made Ash self-sufficient. Being poor made her competitive. In elementary school she competed for better grades than her best friend. In high school she competed at typing and debating for awards and recognition.

Ash felt that her early marriage was another form of competition. Marriage at seventeen made Ash feel "more mature" than her friends.

When Ash discovered selling, it was suited perfectly to her competitive, enthusiastic nature. It began as a way to get a set of books for her three children. Next, it became part-time work to earn extra money. When she divorced in 1945, selling became the means of supporting her children.

Ash realized that as a mother, homemaker, and sole bread-

27

Texas' beauty expert MARY KAY ASH.
— Courtesy of Halcyon Associates, Inc.

winner she had to be organized. She started her day with calls for prospective customers and recruits. Then, after taking care of housework and before her children were home from school, Ash made her deliveries and scheduled her parties.

Following her rule of priorities — God first, family second, and career third — Ash became successful in her career. When her sales at Stanley Home Products averaged $1,000 a month, Ash was named area manager and was offered a job as unit manager covering the entire United States. Because it meant moving every six months, Ash turned down the offer. When she found out that it was not an option, Ash resigned from the company.

Ash felt rejected and angry. How could a company be so indifferent to an employee who had done so much for the company? As she fumed, she made notes. It was a way to vent her anger, and maybe it would help other women in the business world.

After a week of writing, Ash had a list of the problems she had encountered during her years in the world of selling, but she didn't have any solutions. A second look at the list made Ash realize that she had the formula for a perfect company. So Ash decided to form that company. She drew out her savings and enlisted the help of her family.

The next step was finding a product that would add to the success of her company. Cosmetics! A company for women that appealed to women! Cosmetics would be the natural product, and those particular cosmetics that Ash had been using were the ones she wanted to sell.

She had first heard about the cosmetics in 1953, when she was giving a World Gift Party. As she watched the women arriving for the party, Ash was astounded by each one's complexion. No matter what her age, each woman had a young and flawless face. Ash also noticed that each woman brought an empty jar to be refilled after a discussion of which formula she was using.

The formula for the beauty product had started as part of a tanning process by the father of one of the women at the party. After noticing the youthful condition of his hands, the tanner had started working on a skin-care product. He and his daughter had worked together to perfect the formula. Ash bought the beauty formula from the family of its developer.

Realizing the importance of location, Ash rented space for her store in a busy mall in downtown Dallas. In that particular mall were the business offices of several large companies. Almost all of the employees were women. Ash knew the importance of catering to customers' needs. In this case, she gave twenty-minute facials during their lunch hours.

On Friday, September 13, 1963, Ash began her dream company, "Beauty by Mary Kay." She sold cosmetics to women in the mall. She recruited consultants to sell cosmetics to women at home. At the end of their first year of business, "Beauty by Mary Kay" held the first convention. They called it a "seminar" and held it in the company warehouse, decorated with crepe paper and balloons. Ash cooked the meal for 200 people and acted as master of ceremonies to hand out awards.

Ash had learned the importance of conventions when she sold for Stanley Home Products. She had been selling for only three weeks but she wanted to go to the annual convention in Dallas, Texas. She was averaging seven dollars a week in sales and knew that she had a lot to learn. She learned some tips on selling and vowed to gain recognition and the award as top salesman at the next convention. After the ceremony, she told the company president, "Next year I am going to be the 'Queen of Sales.'" And by the next year, she was.

Using the formula she had learned at that convention, Ash set a goal, broke it into small, realistic steps, and told somebody what she was going to do.

The highlight of every year at "Beauty by Mary Kay" is the annual seminar. With catered food, elaborate decorations, and expensive prizes, the seminars have become much more elaborate than that first one.

One thing that has not changed since the first meeting is that Ash personally recognizes outstanding sales consultants and offers encouragement. She said, "I believe that public recognition is the finest form of praise." She feels that praise and recognition are very important because "no matter how much profit a company makes, if it doesn't enrich the lives of its people, that company has failed."

Mary Kay Cosmetics, listed for the second time in 1992 as one of the 100 Best Companies to work for in America, could never be called a failure. Mary Kay Cosmetics is, in fact, a leader. It's one of the first companies to use non-animal testing, one that initiated recycling, among the first cosmetic companies with direct sales to provide retirement and disability, and the first cosmetic company to make the public aware of the dangerous effects of the sun.

Again, the one person to thank for all of that is the vivacious and enthusiastic founder of her own company, Mary Kay Ash.

Chapter 4

They Mastered the Arts

Art for Texas women began as functional design. Scraps of fabric, snipped and stitched into a kaleidoscope of color, kept sleeping families warm. Table linens displayed a variety of fine stitches, and babies were bundled in pastel knitted and crocheted blankets.

Entertainment through music was limited to lullabies and hymns for early Texas women. Those with exceptional voices or musical talent often entertained at social functions. A career in music was as rare as gold-inlaid harpsichords on the Texas frontier.

Entertainment in early Texas often took the form of road shows, with traveling circus groups gaining the number-one spot in popularity. Throughout the summer, performers from all over the world could be seen on the dusty fairgrounds of most Texas towns. Molly Bailey, Texas' own circus woman, took her place among early circus masters such as Ringling and Barnum.

In the late 1800s, immigrants from Europe brought a new interest in painting and sculpting. That a leader among those European sculptors would be a woman came as a surprise to the neighbors of Elisabet Ney's Texas plantation. Although her eccentric behavior was not understood by many, her talent was appreciated by most. Her statues of Sam Houston and Stephen F. Austin took their place in both the Texas Capitol and U.S. Capitol. Wealthy Texans and international celebrities of her time posed for her during their moment of fame.

Early Texas women lacked the education or time to devote to writing. Writers, more than any other artist, found themselves competing in a man's world. Katherine Anne Porter, Texas' first celebrated woman writer, said "courage is the first essential" of an artist.

There were many Texas women who did have the courage it took to follow their dreams and take their place among the artists of their time.

KATHERINE ANNE PORTER

She Captured Texas with Words

She lay on a hard cot, alone and near death in a rented room, while her lover faced death on a battlefield. That was Miranda, a character in *Pale Horse, Pale Rider*. The author, Katherine Anne Porter, had almost died from influenza during the World War I epidemic. She said, "I have never written a story that didn't have a foundation in actual human experience."

Just as Porter brought real-life experiences to her fiction, she sometimes added a touch of fiction to her real life. Born in Indian Creek, Texas, on May 15, 1890, Callie Russell Porter later took her grandmother's name. She sometimes listed her date of birth as 1894, even though her mother had died in 1892. To add to the colorful background she wove for herself, Porter adopted as ancestors William Sidney Porter, who wrote as O.Henry, and Jonathan Boone, brother of frontier statesman Daniel Boone.

In *Old Mortality*, Porter described a plantation-style gentility based on her grandmother's life in the South before she came to Texas. Other stories about Texas depict the lives of poor white southerners, maybe gleaned from her memories of life after her

KATHERINE ANNE PORTER at Indian Creek cemetery, near Brownwood, Texas. Dr. Brooks awarded Porter the honorary doctor of literature degree.
— Courtesy of Dr. Roger L. Brooks,
president of Howard Payne University

grandmother's death in 1901. Her neighbors described that life as "filled with rural hardships and hand-me-downs."

The facts of her first marriage were embroidered over like the tapestries of her short stories. She said she was with a theater company in New Orleans when a member of the audience fell in love with her and persuaded her to marry him. Another time she said that she slipped away from a San Antonio convent to marry, and her classmates combined their allowance to buy her a white dress. Another story was that while in New Orleans, she had married a rich, older man who had locked her up.

The truth was that Porter met John Henry Koontz in Inez, Texas. They were married in Louisiana in a civil ceremony in June of 1906, one month after Porter's sixteenth birthday. The marriage was not the romantic story Porter told. The young couple moved often to follow Koontz's work, and they fought violently.

In 1911 Porter fled from Koontz and New Orleans, not stopping until she stood on the shores of Lake Erie. In Chicago, Porter worked on a newspaper and "went into the movies." She claimed that she went to the movie studio to get a story and was given a job as an actress.

After the movie company returned to the West Coast, Porter performed in Texas. Dressed in homemade costumes, she toured between small towns of Texas and Louisiana singing Scottish ballads. That career ended when Porter developed tuberculosis.

Just as she wove the background of her native Texas into her stories, Porter also used settings from New York, where she lived in 1919.

Mexico and its culture were familiar to Porter too. She had been introduced to that culture when she lived in San Antonio. She made her first trip to Mexico in 1920 and returned several times from 1921 to 1930. Porter sympathized with the poor in Mexico during the Obregón Revolution, which erupted while she was there.

Back in New York, she entertained people with stories of her life in Mexico. Her ability to weave a fanciful story caught the attention of an editor. Hearing her account of a trip to Mexico, Carl Van Doren, editor of *Century Magazine,* suggested that she write it as a story. Porter did just that, weaving the facts into a

35

short fiction piece titled "Maria Concepcion." The short story was published in 1922.

Porter recalled that her interest in writing began at the age of six, when she wrote what she subtitled a "nobell." She did very little writing during the time between that first novel and her first published short story, but Porter felt that all of her life experiences were important to her writing.

"I believe that we are preparing all our lives to be somebody or something even unconsciously. . . . One morning, you wake up and find what you were preparing to be," she said.

A writer was what Porter had been preparing to be. Through her travels, her newspaper writing, and her acting experiences, Porter had gathered the information for her many stories.

Her themes of love and hate in short stories about troubled marriages and troubled families could be firsthand experiences from her own life. Order and disorder ran through her stories in the same way that it had run through her life.

In 1939, Porter's *Pale Horse, Pale Rider* was nominated for an award by the Texas Institute of Letters, founded in 1936 to honor and promote Texas writers. The award was given to J. Frank Dobie for his book *Apache Gold, Yaqui Silver.* On a national level, she received recognition for her writing through honorary degrees and fellowships. In 1952 she was the only woman writer in the United States' delegation to a cultural exposition in Paris sponsored by Congress for Cultural Freedom.

Porter returned to Texas in 1954. She had hoped to set up a room at the University of Texas Library in Austin. She felt slighted when a room was dedicated to Dobie instead. That was when she moved to Maryland, and a room was set up at the University of Maryland for her papers.

In 1941 Porter began to work on character sketches of fellow shipmates from her European voyages. She gathered bits and pieces of her life memories from Mexico, Germany, and from her five-month stay in Bermuda. She wove facts and formed the plot for *Ship of Fools,* based on "the image of the ship of this world on its voyage to eternity."

She had hardly begun to work on the book when she stopped because of the divorce that ended her fourth marriage. She resumed work on the novel in Boulder, Colorado, and over the next thirteen years added and revised.

In 1955 she moved to Connecticut for the privacy she needed for her work.

Her work on *Ship of Fools* stopped again when she needed funds. She lectured at many colleges and universities, including Stanford University, University of Chicago, University of Michigan, University of Liege, University of Virginia, and Washington and Lee University.

In 1961 Porter finished her novel. *Ship of Fools* was published in 1962. The novel, her longest work, was made into a motion picture and won awards both as a book and a movie. In 1966, Porter received the Pulitzer Prize and National Book Award.

In 1976, Porter attended a symposium at Howard Payne University in Brownwood, Texas. She was making plans to have papers donated to that university when she became ill. She returned to Texas in death to be buried beside her mother at Indian Creek. On her gravestone is the motto of her heroine, Mary Queen of Scots: "In my end is my beginning." That motto brings to mind a statement made by Porter in 1953, that "the life of the mind and spirit — the fine arts — are the only things that outlive everything else."

TANYA TUCKER

A Child of Country Music

Country superstar Tanya Tucker has come a long way from her West Texas birthplace. But these days the Seminole native counts the distance in more than miles, Top Ten records, or money. Her twenty-four-year career was a journey of self-discovery. After more than a decade of turbulent voyage, she has reached a peaceful harbor.

The country music establishment has seen a change in Tucker over the past six years. They witnessed the singer who blew into town in 1972 as the "Texas Tornado," a nickname bestowed by the press, go from a wild-natured, party-loving girl to a mature woman. Her new attitude is reflected in all areas of her

TANYA TUCKER has been singing for twenty-five years.
— Courtesy Trifecta Entertainment

life including her choice of songs. After defeating a drug and alcohol problem, Tucker released a workout tape in 1993 and is one of the hardest working singers in country music today with nearly 200 shows a year.

What tamed country music's original wild child? The births of her daughter Presley Tanita in 1989 and her son Beau Grayson in 1991 had a lot to do with it. The children's father is actor Ben Reed. Tucker's decision to raise her children as a single mother caused a collective gasp in conservative Nashville. Tucker maintains that she and Reed would be divorced today if they had married. They remain on friendly terms and are devoted parents.

Her children have given her a new perspective on life. Gone are the wild parties, addictions, and carefree relationships that put her on the cover of more tabloids in the 1970s than most zoos would buy to line their bird cages. Tucker said, "Now my life revolves around my kids. The more you're with a child, the more you think about things you've never thought about before. It sounds corny, but I worry about the environment, schools, drugs — things every mother worries about."

Looking at thirty-six-year-old Tucker, it's hard to believe she's the mother of two, much less a country music legend. The vivacious singer could easily pass for a high school cheerleader, complete with the morning-after-the-big-game hoarse voice. But Tucker, unlike most American teenagers who were going to school dances and football games, attended few high school events. At age thirteen she had a hit single with "Delta Dawn." By age fifteen she had a Grammy nomination and appeared on a *Rolling Stone* magazine cover, a rare occurrence for country artists. While her peers were choosing which college to attend, she was touring with her band, an entourage of publicists, managers, and a road crew.

Just a year after she caught the attention of country music fans with her debut hit "Delta Dawn," she struck Top Ten gold again with the brazen selections "What's Your Mama's Name" and "Blood Red and Going Down." Tucker was well on her way to earning her wild teen image.

In 1975 her greatest hits album was her first album to go gold, selling over a million copies.

Tucker's path toward country music stardom began in Wilcox, Arizona, where she and her older sister, La Costa, would harmonize on favorite country tunes. Both girls loved to sing, and their father sensed that they were good. He decided to try Nashville and moved his family east. Nine-year-old Tanya might not have realized the seriousness of her father's offer, "Would you rather go to school or have a singing career?" Like most youngsters, she jumped at the chance to sing. But she gave up much of her childhood in the bargain.

Former construction worker Beau Tucker literally gambled on his younger daughter's singing ability when he won a game of keno in a Las Vegas casino. He used the money to record a demo tape of Tanya to circulate around Nashville. Her throaty voice caught the attention of the head of Columbia Records, who offered her a record deal. Tanya had no idea at the time what a huge task she had accepted.

In the early 1980s, Tucker's restlessness was reflected in her music. She tried experimenting with her musical style. She switched record companies and recorded an album of rock-and-roll songs that other artists, including her idol Elvis Presley, had made famous. It didn't impress fans or industry critics. The album flopped. "I think it was just a searching period," Tucker said of that phase of her career. "I wasn't leaving country music, because that's my roots." She switched record labels once more, and, this time, she really hit a low point. She left that label and didn't record another album for three years. "I just said, 'Forget it, just forget it. I'm sick of some guy that owns a record label telling me what I want to sing and what I can't sing.'"

When she reappeared on the country music scene, she had a better idea of who she was and the type of music she wanted to record. Drug-free and a single mother, her song choices were more mature, showing a sensitive side that earlier songs lacked.

She scored Top Ten hits with heartfelt love songs like "Love Me Like You Used To," "Strong Enough to Bend," and "Two Sparrows in a Hurricane." She could still wring a teardrop out of the most hard-hearted listener with tales of heartbreak like "What Do I Do With Me?," "Some Kind of Trouble," and "Soon." In 1995, she is back on the charts with top-selling records. Her two most recent albums have sold well over a million copies each. Tucker is Liberty Record's top-selling female artist and second only to label-mate Garth Brooks in album sales.

Her second try at success is just as sweet as it was the first time, without the luxury of spare time to savor it. She says she is working as hard as she can to make a comfortable living so she can slow down later and spend time with her children. Tucker may be able to reclaim the title of "Texas Tornado" — this time for her hectic schedule. During 1993 she performed 125 tour dates in the United States and Canada. She released "Tanya Tucker Country Workout," a low-impact aerobics video, and earned two awards for her music videos: Academy of Country Music's Video of the Year and Country Music Television's Female Video Artist of the Year. She also appeared in the 1994 Super Bowl halftime performance. Tanya has secured her place as one of the top five women in country music, along with Dolly Parton, Loretta Lynn, Tammy Wynette, and Kitty Wells.

Tucker does her part for charity, too, serving as the ambassador for the National Multiple Sclerosis Society, and she helps the St. Jude's Children's Hospital in Memphis.

Tucker's ambition is to keep singing and performing, but these days she has an important reason to continue her journey: "My goal is to be with my kids and raise my family."

Molly Ivins

Politically Irreverent

Molly Ivins has never found it easy to be a liberal, feminist, outspoken, six-foot-tall gal in a conservative, macho, redneck state like Texas. Fortunately, she didn't let it get her down. In fact, she decided her life, as well as life in general, was quite hilarious, and so she began to write about it.

Ivins has been called plenty of things besides a liberal. Some politicians call her the thorn in their side, but many newspaper readers declare her a ray of sunshine in an otherwise gloomy political landscape. As a Texan, Ivins is most comfortable being a "good ol' girl" who calls it like she sees it. Regardless of what others call her, most everyone agrees Ivins is the funniest political and cultural writer since Will Rogers.

Columnist MOLLY IVINS mixes humor with prose.
— Courtesy of Molly Ivins

Politics is not usually a humorous topic. It is a subject that divides people. Good manners suggest that politics as a conversation topic is best avoided. But Ivins throws caution to the wind and openly examines politics, especially the Texas variety. Political foibles have been her writing subject for most of her career. As a writer she's determined to get others to see politics her way: it's better to laugh than to cry. And between the tongue and cheek of Ivins' wit, readers of her column learn the facts about state and national political issues.

In the preface to her second book, *Nothin' But Good Times Ahead*, Ivins writes that she hopes her collection of columns "will remind you that we need to stop and laugh along the way. We live in a Great Nation, but those who attempt to struggle through it unarmed with a sense of humor are apt to wind up in my Aunt Eula's Fort Worth Home for the Terminally Literal-Minded, gibbering like some demented neoconservative about the Decline of Civilization."

Ivins is living proof that the expression "laugh and the world laughs with you" is on the mark. She's been chuckling and writing about political shenanigans for over twenty years. Currently a syndicated columnist writing for the *Fort Worth Star-Telegram*, Ivins is the author of two books, including the national best-seller *Molly Ivins Can't Say That, Can She?*

She got her first taste of political writing during her early years as a journalist working for the *Minneapolis Tribune* during the turbulent 1960s. Her assignment was to report on racial issues and the feminist movement among other social changes of the day. Inspired by the social change she witnessed in the North, Ivins returned to Texas in 1970 to enlighten her own state by coediting the *Texas Observer*. While working for this political magazine, Ivins had her introduction to the Texas legislature. Politics became her subject and six years of reporting the antics of the Lone Star state's lawmakers set her comical writing style in concrete. With her wit and ability to get the Texas twang across in print, Ivins is not like the average political columnist.

Kaye Northcott was Ivins' coeditor at the *Texas Observer*, and she feels that Ivins' contribution to Texas has been positive. Northcott said that her columns have added a humorous perspective to Texas politics. "I think Molly has done that (lightened) for a lot of Texas liberals. . . . She makes people feel right and good about what they do."

Sam Hudson has known Ivins since her *Texas Observer* days and says her strength as a political columnist lies in the fact that she "still lives in the same country that her readers live in. She always sees that politics is real and has real results in the thumpable American Republic."

Born in Monterey, California, in 1944, Ivins grew up in East Texas when her parents moved the family to Houston in 1948. Her traditionally conservative parents gave her a conventional upbringing, but she grew up to be a liberal. Since a liberal in Texas is about as comfortable as a rabbit at a dog show, Ivins longed for the sophistication she knew could only be found in the East. After high school graduation she headed to Massachusetts to attend Smith College. Ivins earned a bachelor's degree in history and spent a year in Paris studying politics at the Institute of Political Sciences. When she returned to the United States she enrolled at Columbia University in New York City to earn a master's degree in journalism.

Along the way, Ivins found that northerners aren't nearly as open-minded as she had believed. Her informal style of reporting often got her into trouble. She worked for the *New York Times* for six years covering state politics, but by 1982 it was back to Texas and a readership that appreciated her down-home way of reporting the facts — most of the time. She once wrote about a Dallas-area congressman, speculating, "If his IQ slips any lower, we'll have to water him twice a day." In the fallout, including advertiser boycotts and subscription cancellations, her employers at the *Dallas Times-Herald* backed her completely.

Fortunately for Ivins she was employed by the more liberal of the two Metroplex newspapers, but the *Times-Herald* went bankrupt in 1991, leaving Ivins temporarily out of work. She barely missed a beat as she signed on with the nearby *Fort Worth Star-Telegram* in 1992.

Her extensive free-lance writing includes articles on women's issues, politics, and the Texas mystique for *Mother Jones, The Nation, Ms., Atlantic, Esquire,* and *TV Guide.*

Ivins has received numerous journalism awards during her career and was named Outstanding Alumna by Columbia University's School of Journalism in 1976. A three-time finalist for the Pulitzer Prize, she won Texas' Headliners Award for the state's best column in 1993.

True to form, Ivins relishes the absurd, pointing out that one of her greatest honors was that she "was once banned from the campus of Texas A&M (University)." So take a tip from Ivins: When politics has you weary, find her column in your newspaper's editorial section or open up one of her books. A good laugh puts everything into perspective.

Chapter 5

They Took to the Skies

ENGINE-DRIVEN MACHINE GLIDES ABOVE DUNES AT KITTY HAWK! In 1903 the message was not front-page news. The birth of aviation was probably the least heralded historic event since the discovery of the wheel.

Orville and Wilbur Wright's historic twelve-second flight was the culmination of four years of trial and error which began in 1899 when the brothers decided to tackle the age-old question: Will men fly?

By 1908 aviation supporters were convincing others to give flying a chance. Lt. Benjamin Foulois made the first military flight on March 2, 1910, and in 1915 was sent to San Antonio to organize the first aero squadron to help end bandit uprisings along the Texas-Mexico border. Later, San Antonio was a center for training World War I pilots.

Flying took America by storm. Men and women across the country enrolled in aviation courses. Flying was seen by many young men and women as an exciting way to make both a living and, perhaps, a name for themselves.

Barnstorming provided entertainment for rural families who flocked to the aerial exhibitions. For a quarter they could experience flight by taking a ride in a biplane.

Texas provided ideal weather conditions and flat terrain for airstrips. Over the years Texas played a bigger role in aviation as numerous air bases were established across the state.

During World War II, Texas became the site of a historic program when the Women Air Service Pilots (WASPs) were based at Avenger Field in Sweetwater. WASPs were trained for noncombat flying duties to free male pilots for heavy air campaigns in Europe and the Pacific.

After a seven-month training program, 1,074 women served in the Army Air Force by towing target sleeves for gunnery practice and ferrying new planes to bases. Many WASPs died during training and in service when faulty planes crashed. Because they were not military personnel, they were not covered by military benefits.

It took thirty-four years before legislation was signed into law recognizing the Women Air Service Pilots' contributions to the war. It would be fifty years before Congress granted women the honor to serve their country as combat pilots.

KATHERINE STINSON

A Flying Family

"Texas is the ideal location for a flying school," he shouted over the roar of the plane's engine. "They say it's warm nearly ten months of the year in the southern part of the state. Bring up the nose a little as you come in for a landing."

The young pilot nodded and pulled up on the biplane's control column. There was a rustling sound and gentle slapping against the airplanes' belly as the craft lost altitude and cropped the topmost branches of a stand of oak trees. Seconds later, the plane touched down in a freshly mowed field.

Newspaper reporters and photographers sprinted toward the plane as it rolled to a stop. "Max, can you tell us about the plans to move your school to Texas?" shouted a reporter from the *Huntsville Times.*

47

The "Flying School Girl," KATHERINE STINSON.
— Courtesy of Stinson Airfield

One man shouted, "What's this we hear about a new pilot soloing after just four hours of flying?"

"Well, boys, it's your lucky day," Max Lillie announced as he stood up in the plane. "My newest protege and quick study happens to be sitting in the cockpit."

Max Lillie was as well known for his showmanship as he was for his nationally respected flying school. "I'll let my pilot answer any questions you have."

Pushing up out of the biplane, the small, lean pilot rested atop the cockpit seat, adjusting a pair of goggles and loosening the chin strap of a well-worn flying helmet.

"Tell me, why'd you take up the dangerous business of flying?"

"Well, to tell you the truth, I never stopped to consider the dangers," the pilot answered in a soprano voice. "My mother never warned me not to do this or that for fear of being hurt."

A chubby hand waved above a sea of fedoras. "How did you learn to fly so quickly? I mean, four days is some kinda record, kid!" The reporter stuffed a soggy cigar into his mouth.

"I decided I'd better learn to fly before Mr. Lillie changed his mind about teaching me," the pilot said and tugged the leather cap off. A cascade of black curls fell around her shoulders.

Flashes of light blinded her as half a dozen cameras shot off. Katherine Stinson was overwhelmed. She had heard of the attention pilots received, but she wasn't prepared for instant fame.

Fame had come practically overnight for the farm girl from the Deep South. It had been less than six weeks since her first flight and only weeks since she earned her license.

Newspaper headlines chronicled her accomplishments: STINSON FOURTH WOMAN PILOT IN THE WORLD. She had proudly accepted her pilot's license from the Federation Aeronautique Internationale. Katherine was still amazed by the fact that she had almost missed her opportunity to be a pilot.

As a girl growing up in Mississippi, Katherine had two passions — music and flying. It was her love of music that made a career in aviation a reality. Katherine decided to get her pilot's license to earn money to study music in Europe. The nineteen-year-old had heard that pilots could earn $1,000 a day. Once her parents' approval was secured, Katherine began her search for an instructor. It took two years to find one.

49

Max Lillie, a well-known aviator from Chicago, was one of only 200 licensed pilots in the world. He was also skeptical about the diminutive girl's ability to fly an airplane.

Barely five feet tall and only 100 pounds, Katherine had to do some big talking to convince Lillie that she could handle a plane. Lillie's worries proved unfounded. Katherine took to airplanes like an eagle takes to the skies. In July of 1912 she began. After just four hours of flying, she soloed (flew alone). By July 12, 1912, she was a licensed pilot.

Soon after receiving her license, Katherine was entertaining crowds at air shows. The "Flying School Girl" wowed her audiences with daring loop-the-loops and a stunt she invented called the "Dippy Twist Loop," in which she performed loops with wing over wing flips.

Her fearlessness earned her many records. She was the first woman to perform a loop-the-loop and the first pilot to skywrite at night. She achieved this first by skywriting "CAL" with fireworks at a centennial celebration in Los Angeles.

By 1913 Katherine was making headlines as well as the income she had heard pilots could earn. Now she could afford that trip to Europe. By then she had set a new course; music was still a passion, but flying was her life.

That same year Katherine and her family moved to San Antonio at Max Lillie's request. He convinced them that San Antonio's mild winters were perfect for year-round flying.

The Texas city was on its way to becoming a national aviation center. Pioneers like Lillie and Stinson did their part to introduce the modern form of transportation there.

In the early 1900s, though, San Antonio's destiny as an aviation hub was several decades and two world wars away. In 1913, the only thing aviators cared about was the ideal climate.

Katherine and her mother followed Lillie to San Antonio, moving their own flying school from Hot Springs, Arkansas. They were allowed to use the airstrip at Fort Sam Houston, where Lt. Benjamin Foulois did flight tests.

Her sister and brothers, Marjorie, Eddie, and Jack, taught flying while Katherine appeared in air shows around the country. Marjorie trained eighty pilots for service in World War I when the school moved to a larger airfield in 1915.

Katherine's flying exhibitions supported the school while she continued to set speed and distance records. She amazed British crowds by circling the House of Parliament and St. Paul's Cathedral.

In 1916 she traveled to Japan, where 25,000 adoring fans turned out to watch her fly over Tokyo. While in Asia she made a private appearance in China for the country's leaders.

At the start of World War I, Katherine and Marjorie volunteered to fly for their country, but both were turned down because they were women. Katherine eventually found a way to serve in the war by driving an ambulance in London and France. While serving in Europe, she contracted tuberculosis. The disease ended her flying career, and in 1928 she retired to New Mexico for the warm climate. There she met and married Miguel Otero, Jr., a former World War I airman. Katherine lived in New Mexico until her death in 1977.

Katherine and her family are remembered by the city they flew over so many times. The airfield where they trained many Texas pilots still bears their family name. Not far from Stinson Field in southwest San Antonio is Katherine Stinson Middle School. Junior high students walking past the school's display case can read about and see pictures of Texas' "Flying School Girl," an aviation pioneer.

BESSIE COLEMAN

Brave Bessie

"I am right on the threshold of opening a school," Bessie Coleman wrote in a letter to her sister, Elois, in the spring of 1926. An aviation school for black men and women was a dream Bessie had nurtured since she became the first black woman pilot in the world.

She had already overcome many obstacles in her pursuit to "amount to something," and she wanted to uplift her race. Growing up poor and black in the rural South made fulfilling any dream a hard-fought battle.

BESSIE COLEMAN, first black woman pilot, was known as "Brave Bessie."
— Courtesy of Marion Coleman

Bessie was born on January 26, 1892, in Atlanta, Texas, to Susan and George Coleman. Two years later the family moved to Waxahachie, thirty miles south of Dallas. There, her father bought a small plot of land to farm. As the oldest daughter, Bessie cared for her siblings while her parents planted and picked cotton.

Life was never easy, but it got more difficult when George, who was part Indian, decided to move to Oklahoma's Indian Territory, where he had more rights. He tried to persuade his wife and family to go with him, but Susan was determined to stay in Texas.

Susan found a housecleaning job with a white family in Waxahachie. She also took in laundry and picked cotton during harvest season. The children picked cotton alongside their mother. Bessie assumed more responsibility for her younger brothers and sisters, missing school when her mother needed her at home.

Bessie's mother encouraged her children to learn, borrowing books from a wagon library for them to read. Bessie learned about black leaders Harriet Tubman and Booker T. Washington while observing her own mother's quality of quiet pride. Susan was a religious woman who felt that in God's eyes all people were equal. She gave Bessie the self-confidence needed to achieve her goals despite the hardship of being a black woman in the early 1900s.

Bessie graduated from high school and used the money she earned doing laundry to enroll in the Colored Agricultural and Normal University in Langston, Oklahoma. After one term her money ran out and she went back to Waxahachie. She knew if she was going to "amount to something" she needed to get away from the racist oppression of the South. She went to Chicago to live with her brother and his family. Seeking a job that would offer her a chance to better herself, Bessie settled on being a manicurist in Duncan's Barber Shop on State Street.

Five years after Bessie arrived in Chicago, she decided she would learn to fly. She applied to and was turned down by several aviation schools before she talked to her friend Robert Abbott, publisher of Chicago's respected black newspaper, the *Chicago Defender*. He convinced Bessie to study French and apply to

French aviation schools because they were more liberal in their attitude toward women and blacks.

On November 20, 1920, Bessie boarded a ship bound for France to study aviation at the Ecole d'Aviation des Freres Coudron at Le Crotoy in the Somme. She completed a seven-month program to earn her pilot's license in June 1921, making her the first American black woman licensed to fly anywhere in the world. She later made another trip to France for more training.

On September 3, 1922, Bessie made her first American flying exhibition, heralded in a New York newspaper as the "first public flight of a black woman in this country." Six weeks later "Brave Bessie," as she had been christened, flew in an air show at the Checkerboard Airdrome in Chicago. Both shows attracted thousands of curious spectators, black and white, who were impressed by her flying skills as well as her dramatic flair. She dressed in a military-style uniform complete with epaulets and a Sam Browne belt that was custom-made in Paris.

The next few years were busy as Bessie traveled the United States for exhibitions and speaking engagements in movie theaters and churches. Her lectures included accounts of her training in Europe and her flying experiences, but she always encouraged the members of her race to become pilots. All her efforts and finances were directed toward her goal to open a flying school.

In early 1923 Bessie was making strides toward her goal. She had opened an office for her school in Chicago. One of her students was the advertising manager for a California tire company, the Coast Tire and Rubber Company. Bessie talked with him about dropping the company's advertising pamphlets from an airplane. The student and his employer liked the idea, so Bessie headed for California in late January. She was scheduled to fly an exhibition in early February 1923, but her plane crashed shortly after takeoff from Santa Monica. The motor quit, and the plane nose-dived 300 feet. Unconscious, Bessie was pulled from the demolished Jenny and hospitalized with a broken leg, fractured ribs, and multiple lacerations on her face. She left California four months later with no airplane, no job prospects, and no money, but she still had her dream to open an aviation school for blacks.

"The Negro race is the only race without aviators, and I want to interest the Negro in flying and thus help the best way I'm equipped in to uplift the colored race," Bessie was quoted as saying by the *Houston Post-Dispatch* in May 1925. It had been two years since her crash in California, and Bessie was back on the flying circuit, determined to rebuild her dream. She told the Houston newspaper her goal was "to make Uncle Tom's cabin into a hangar by establishing a flying school."

Her Texas exhibitions were a success, and she was invited to visit with the state's governor, Miriam A. "Ma" Ferguson, after a show in Austin.

On a tour of speaking engagements and flying exhibitions in the South to raise funds for her school, Bessie was giving lectures in Orlando, Florida, when she was befriended by the Reverend Hezakiah Hill and his wife, Viola. They persuaded Bessie to open a beauty shop in Orlando to earn a steady income. She promised the Hills she would give up dangerous exhibition flying to lecture and teach. But she had one last scheduled engagement for a Memorial Day show in Jacksonville, Florida, for the Negro Welfare League.

On April 29, 1926, Bessie visited every black public school in Jacksonville. That night she spoke at the Strand Theater. The next day she and mechanic William D. Wills took her newly acquired Jenny up so she could check on adequate landing sites for a parachute jump she would make during the show. Bessie was not wearing a seat belt because she needed to look over the side of the plane. They circled at 2,000 feet, then climbed to 3,500 feet. The Jenny accelerated abruptly, then nose-dived and went into a tailspin at 1,000 feet. It flipped upside down at 500 feet. Bessie fell out and landed "with a sickening thud" 100 yards north at the far end of Paxon Field, the airport they were circling. Wills could not regain control of the plane and crashed about 1,000 feet from where Bessie fell. Investigators later determined the plane crashed because a wrench, left in the plane, jammed its gears.

Bessie's body was transported to Chicago, where a military escort of the African American Eighth Infantry Regiment of the Illinois National Guard took the coffin to a southside funeral home. An estimated 10,000 people viewed her coffin before it was moved on May 7, 1926, to the Pilgrim Baptist Church for the funeral. Pastor Junius C. Austin eulogized Bessie, saying, "This girl was one hundred years ahead of the race she loved so well and by whom she was least appreciated."

Over fifty years would pass before Bessie's legacy would be officially recognized by her race and the city of Chicago. Mayor Richard Daley renamed a road at O'Hare Airport "Bessie Coleman Drive" in 1980. In February 1992, for Black History Month, the Chicago City Council requested that the United States Postal Service issue a stamp "commemorating Bessie Coleman and her singular accomplishment in becoming the world's first African American pilot and, by definition, an American legend." In 1994 the Postal Service announced that a stamp would be issued in her honor.

Some blacks, mostly pilots, had always held Bessie's legacy in high regard. Lt. William J. Powell, founder of the Aero Clubs named in Bessie's honor, dedicated his 1934 book, *Black Wings,* to her memory: "Because of Bessie Coleman we have overcome that which was much worse than racial barriers. We have overcome the barriers within ourselves and dared to dream."

KARA HULTGREEN

Pioneering Combat Pilot

The last few notes of taps fade as navy commander Harry Ennis presents a U.S. flag to Sally Spears. Spears wipes her eyes with the handkerchief she has been clutching since the memorial service started. Muffled sobs from the crowd of family and friends are drowned out by the squadron of F-14 jets overhead. One plane drops out of formation for the missing-man tribute. Today's flyover is historical as well as sentimental because it honors the first woman pilot: Navy Lt. Kara Hultgreen, Spears' daughter.

It had been four days since Hultgreen's F-14 crashed in the Pacific Ocean on approach for landing aboard the USS *Abraham Lincoln.* Carrier-based landings require precision to bring a 55,000-pound F-14 Tomcat down on a 100-foot-wide, moving tar-

Pioneer combat pilot Navy Lt. KARA HULTGREEN
poses beside the Navy's F-14 Tomcat.

— Courtesy of U.S. Navy

get at speeds of 150 miles per hour. If all conditions are not right, the control tower advises the pilot to circle and try again. Hultgreen's plane was leaning to one side, and she veered off to try her approach again when the plane began to roll left. Radar Intercept Officer Lt. Matthew Klemish ejected before the plane hit the water. He was rescued, but searchers in helicopters and ships were not able to find Hultgreen. She was presumed dead, missing in action.

Her mother will never forget October 26, 1994. That's the day a navy officer and a chaplain came to Spears' home to tell her that Kara, twenty-nine, had crashed at 3:01 P.M. Tuesday, October 25, and was lost at sea. "Not Kara," she shook her head in disbelief, as tears welled up. "Not Kara."

Both mother and daughter knew the risks Hultgreen accepted as a jet pilot. It was a fact they had lived with for seven years when Hultgreen decided to pursue a career as a pilot. They didn't discuss the danger Kara faced each time she flew. When Spears talked to her daughter two days before the crash, the topic of their conversation was computers. "We never talked about the danger. It was just always a fact — that it was dangerous. I never thought it would happen to Kara. She was careful. She was smart. She was prepared. She was very directed in the pursuit of her goals," her mother said.

Hultgreen's dream of being a pilot was a lifetime in the making. As a kid, she was fascinated by aviation, especially space exploration. She wanted to be an astronaut. When she found there were only two ways to become an astronaut — to either earn a doctorate in science or become a navy test pilot — she decided to choose the more exciting route of pilot. "I was an adventurous kid. I always liked speed," she once said.

Hultgreen loved to fly, and it showed, literally. Every photograph taken of her with jets showed an exuberant pilot with a big grin on her face. Her enthusiasm for flying was evident in every interview she gave, whether to hometown newspapers or national magazines. "I can't believe I get paid to do this," she said.

Hultgreen graduated from the University of Texas at Austin in 1987 with a degree in aerospace engineering. Then it was off to Navy Officers' Candidate School for a fourteen-week training program. Although Officers' Candidate School had been tough, it was nothing compared to primary flight training in Corpus Christi. Hultgreen admitted she was intimidated at first since she had never flown, but she learned quickly. "I used to call my mom and say, 'Oh, my God, I can't taxi this thing,'" she said. "A week later she would ask if I was still having trouble. By then I could have taxied all the way to San Antonio."

Hultgreen became an accomplished pilot, attended jet school, earned her wings, and trained ships' crews to shoot down enemy planes as a member of a tactical squadron. She found it frustrating that, as a woman, she would not be able to fly combat planes even though she was as well trained as the male pilots. A limit was put on how far she could advance as a pilot and an officer in the navy because of the combat exclusion law that said women could not fly fighter jets.

Hultgreen and others wrote to lawmakers and testified at a congressional hearing in an effort to repeal the law. In April 1993 the Pentagon ended combat restrictions for female pilots, and Hultgreen was assigned to Fighter Squadron 213, the Blacklions, at Miramar Naval Air Station in San Diego. She began training in May 1993 to learn to fly the navy's oldest combat jet, the F-14 Tomcat. In July 1994 she qualified as a combat pilot by completing training and successful night landings on the USS *Constellation.*

Landing the F-14 at night proved to be the most difficult part of training. "During the day it's a Mardi Gras," Hultgreen said. Landings at night were a different story. The nerve-wracking job of lining up the plane and snagging the cable must be achieved using navigation instruments. Many pilots have been disqualified because they couldn't get the hang of night landings. The navy is cautious, making sure that pilots are well trained in landings on aircraft carriers. Hultgreen was disqualified on her first attempt at night landings, but she went back, practiced, and qualified on her second attempt.

Spears said her daughter was uncomfortable with the media attention given to her because she was a female fighter pilot. "Kara just wanted to fly. She wanted to be thought of as a pilot, just like the men in the squadron." Her goal was to be the best pilot she could be.

Ironically, the fact that she was a woman pilot has led to questions about the crash and her ability as a pilot. In the weeks that followed Hultgreen's crash, rumors spread that she was unqualified to fly the F-14 despite average to above average ratings by instructors. According to a story in *Newsweek* magazine, "Someone within the Navy sent out anonymous faxes falsifying Hultgreen's flying record."

But eyewitnesses aboard the USS *Abraham Lincoln* said they saw visual evidence that the plane was experiencing mechanical problems. Flight deck crew members reported seeing smoke from the rear of the plane. One wing tilted as the plane came closer to the ship. Scott Watkins, senior editor of *Women Pilot*, visited the *Lincoln* several days after the crash to do a story on flight deck operations. He said crew members who spoke to him were convinced Hultgreen took action to keep the jet from crashing into the ship's deck. "It appeared to them that she pulled the aircraft away from the ship," Watkins said. "One eyewitness said, 'She sacrificed herself to save the ship.'"

In the days following the crash, navy officials announced they would try to retrieve the plane which lay nearly 4,000 feet below the ocean's surface. Once they had the plane, a full investigation could determine the cause of the crash.

During a search for the F-14 jet in November 1994, an unmanned robotic submarine discovered Hultgreen's body fifty feet from the jet. It took the submarine ninety minutes to bring up the body. The next day the navy used cranes to carefully recover the downed jet in one piece. Following an inspection, there may be answers to the questions, including the one asked by the pilot's family and friends: "Why?"

The immaculate grounds of Arlington National Cemetery are the final resting place for Navy Lt. Kara Hultgreen. She received a soldier's burial for being America's first fallen female combat pilot.

Chapter 6

They Became Politicians

Texas women had an interest in politics long before they had the right to vote. They campaigned and cajoled to make sure the right man got into office.

After getting the vote, they voted themselves into office. Not only were they voted in, they were appointed, with thirty-two women on state boards and commissions.

Were women being appeased? Were they acting as puppets for the men? For whatever reason the door of politics was opened to women, they took advantage of the opportunity to get into the public buildings and high offices of the state. And once they had gotten their foot in the door, women continued to fight for other legal rights that were still forbidden to them.

In 1954, Sarah T. Hughes introduced the bill in the Texas legislature that gave women the right to serve on juries. In 1969, married women could own property for the first time. In 1973, in a constitutional amendment, women received full equal rights for the first time in Texas.

An all-woman supreme court, appointed in 1925 by Governor Pat Neff, was so named only because the men were disqualified due to a conflict of interest. But even though they served only one case, they conducted business as usual with a professionalism equal that of men.

Miriam A. "Ma" Ferguson ran for governor only because her husband Jim had created a public scandal. But she increased aid to education, mental health, and welfare. She also passed anti-Klan laws and pardoned thousands of prisoners. Another woman, Ann Richards, would serve as governor of Texas in a new era, and Barbara Jordan would break down barriers of all kinds to serve her state.

BARBARA JORDAN

Making a Change

John Patten, one of the black convicts pardoned by Governor Miriam Ferguson, was released on "full and unconditional pardon." Barbara Jordan, born February 21, 1936, twelve years after his release, was Patten's favorite granddaughter. She helped him with his junk business, and he gave her a philosophy about rising above the accepted "black woman's place" of her time.

He taught her to be independent, saying, "You just trot your own horse and don't get into the same rut as everyone else." Jordan stayed out of the ruts.

In high school she joined the debate team, unconventional for girls at that time. She decided to become a lawyer after hearing Chicago attorney Edith Sampson speak at Career Day. Law was a profession open mostly to whites and males.

Grandpa Patten told Jordan, "Do your best." She decided early in life that she did not want to be ordinary. After she won the 1952 National United Ushers Association Oratorical Contest, Jordan told newspaper reporters for the Houston *Informer*, "It's just another milestone I have passed: it's just the beginning."

At Texas Southern University in Houston, Jordan continued debating, winning first place at the Southern Forensic Conference at Baylor University in Waco. She tied the Harvard Debate Team in 1954.

Jordan gained admission to Boston University Law School. It was there Barbara discovered that in education "separate was not equal." Having her ideas challenged for the first time and

*BARBARA JORDAN, former congresswoman, taught public affairs
at the University of Texas.*
— Courtesy of University of Texas Institute of Texan Cultures

63

competing with students more knowledgeable in the law profession, Jordan felt that she was finally being educated.

Jordan remembered that Grandpa Patten had said, "Just remember the world is not a playground, but a schoolroom. Life is not a holiday, but an education." Boston University was the schoolroom where she gathered her knowledge of law. Later, Jordan entered the political arena as though she were entering a schoolroom. "She always did her homework" was how one colleague described Barbara's preparation for the Senate.

Grandpa Patten taught by example that one can overcome hardships in life. Jordan learned early that growing up black was a definite hardship. She learned about prejudice when she left the protection of her family and community to travel with the debate team. She learned that black people were not welcome in restaurants, motels, and restrooms across the southern United States.

Jordan refused to let racial prejudice ruin her chances to use her talent and intelligence. Seeing that the Supreme Court ruling against segregation in 1954 was not going to happen overnight, Jordan realized that "someone had to push integration along in a private way if it were ever going to come."

Jordan felt that the people who could push integration had to be the "black people who could make it in this white man's world." Grandpa Patten had taught Jordan that she could make it in anybody's world.

Making her way in the world of law was slow at first. Clients were scarce among the poor, all-black community. In her free time Jordan volunteered on the Harris County Democratic Committee and became vice-chairman. She was elected president of the all-black Houston Law Association, even though she was the only woman member. She served on the Houston Council on Human Relations.

Working on the Kennedy/Johnson presidential campaign, Jordan was bitten by the political bug and ran for the state senate. Losing in 1962 and 1964, she decided to ally herself with other black politicians to gain a bloc vote. That and redistricting of senate delegates helped her win a seat on the Texas Senate.

Time magazine called the election of Barbara Jordan and Curtis M. Graves to the state senate a "quiet change" in Texas politics when "capable Negro office seekers win white support necessary for victory."

By the time she won her second term in 1968, Jordan had the support of many powerful Texas politicians, including Lyndon B. Johnson. President Johnson invited her to Washington to discuss a fair-housing bill and appointed her to a special economic commission.

In 1972 she received the distinction of being the first black woman to head a state government when she served as Texas governor for a day when the governor and attorney general were both away.

Being the first black woman from Texas to be elected to the United States Congress was another milestone for Jordan. Assigned to the House Judiciary Committee, Jordan was soon thrown into the national spotlight with the impeachment hearings for President Richard Nixon. In her "We the people" speech, Barbara got the attention of the people with the rhythm of her words. She brought new light to the words of the most honored of American documents.

On July 12, 1976, at Madison Square Garden, she again exhibited her talent at oratory when she spoke at the Democratic Convention. The delegates had continued to mill about the convention hall and converse among themselves during the first speech. The committee chairman told her to speak to the television audience because the delegates would not be listening. "One hundred, forty-four years ago," she said in her commanding style. The delegates did listen, riveted to every word as she continued, "But there is something different about tonight. . . . I, Barbara Jordan, am a keynote speaker."

Barbara was in awe of the fact that her presence was evidence that the American dream of equality for all was nearer. From injustices to herself and her family to *Brown vs. the Board of Education of Topeka* and on to the Civil Rights Act of 1964, Barbara had seen that equality nearing and she had helped give it the needed push.

In 1979 the time had come for Jordan to move in another direction. Instead of running for a fourth congressional term, Jordan accepted a professorship at the University of Texas in Austin. In her "Political Values and Ethics" course at the Lyndon

B. Johnson School of Public Affairs, Jordan passed on those lessons learned at Grandpa Patten's knee — his "gospel according to St. John," as he called them.

One lesson Jordan taught is that it is a matter of deciding on the ethical thing to do, not just the legal. She felt it necessary for politicians, acting in the interest of others, to follow a higher ethical standard than those in other professions, who act in their own interests.

Another lesson that she taught was, "If you're dissatisfied with the way things are, then you have got to resolve to change them."

As she told students at Texas Southern University, "We must exchange a philosophy of excuses — what I am is beyond my control — for the philosophy of responsibility. A man of liberty does not burn down the neighborhood store, then beg for supper."

Jordan, appointed by President Bill Clinton to the Commission on Immigration Reform, continued to campaign for the rights of all Americans. And she continued to receive recognition for her efforts. The Sara Lee Corporation honored her with the Frontrunner Award as one of America's exceptional women in 1994. They recognized her because "she leads by example — as ethics guru and teacher."

One lesson that Barbara Jordan taught through example is that anyone can accomplish a goal. She said, "I believe that I get from the soil and the spirit of Texas the feeling that I, as an individual, can accomplish whatever I want to. . . . I like that spirit."

That was the kind of spirit her Grandpa Patten had passed on to her. Jordan said, "He had given me a God who did not say bend your knee and await a better day, strength to believe in myself and my intelligence, and a guarantee that he would always be there for me."

Just as Grandpa Patten had always been there for her, Barbara Jordan was always there for the black community, for women, and for all Americans. As a politician, a teacher, and a strong citizen, she was there to help make her country a better place until her death on January 17, 1996. Ann Richards, in an article in the *Austin American-Statesman,* voiced the feelings of many when she said, "America has lost a patriot, a trail-blazer, a hero."

ANN RICHARDS

Governor Ann

Ann Richards climbed into the "Good Ol' Boy" tree house of Texas politics, took over the club, and tore down the "NO GIRLS ALLOWED" sign as the state's second woman governor.

She did it with a mixture of gumption, old-fashioned hard work, and political savvy all held together with an ample dose of moxie.

During her first year in office, Richards appointed more women, blacks, and Hispanics to state positions than any governor before her. Those appointments were part of her campaign platform termed a "New Texas," which would better represent the state's people.

Crime decreased and business prospered while Richards stuck by her promise of "no new taxes." But when it came time to run for a second term as governor, Richards lost to her Republican opponent.

Her governorship began when she took the oath of office on January 15, 1991. She may not have been the first woman to hold the state's highest elected position, but she was definitely the first woman to govern the state. And she brought her unique style to the job.

The first woman governor, Miriam A. Ferguson, entered the race at her husband's request and deferred to him for the duration of her governorship. James Ferguson, Jr., was governor from 1915 until his impeachment in 1917, when he was barred from ever again holding public office.

Ann Richards has never been one to sit back and let others make the decisions. From her first taste of politics as a high school junior to her first public office as a Travis County commissioner, she tackled every challenge and learned from every experience.

As with other women of her generation, Richards grew up believing that a woman's role was wife and mother. But Richards had one trait that was as deeply ingrained as her Texas roots; she had an opinion and expressed it eloquently. Speaking was a tal-

*ANN RICHARDS was Texas' second woman governor,
its first "billion-dollar treasurer."*

— Courtesy of Ann Richards

ent she inherited from her yarn-spinning father. From the time she entered grade school, Richards realized she had a knack for holding a group's attention when she spoke. Years of expression lessons honed that skill.

Her love of speaking continued through high school and into college. She won first place in the doubles debate in state competition her senior year. In 1950 she earned a speech scholarship to Baylor University, where she continued to practice persuasive speaking. When she discovered that the men's debate team would be attending a competition in the East, Richards convinced her debate sponsor to allow the women's team to attend their own competition. That was the first time her speaking ability took her places. Public speaking became her claim to fame.

Her witticisms, delivered with a lilting Texas drawl, won her many supporters and disarmed her opponents. America got a dose of Ann Richards when she stepped into the national political spotlight to deliver the keynote address at the 1988 Democratic Convention. Her speech, irreverent but moving, made her a national celebrity. In her address, she urged voters to think of the future for their children and grandchildren.

Richards' reputation rose after the speech. She became a nationally known politician. But most Americans, Texans included, didn't know what to make of the silver-haired grandmother. The Harley-Davidson riding, pheasant-hunting governor is as unorthodox as they come. Down-home and city smart, Richards epitomizes Texas — as colorful as a Panhandle sunset, as determined as an Alamo defender, and as full of contrast as the Lone Star state itself.

Richards got her first glimpse into government when she was selected to attend Girls State in Austin her junior year of high school. "Girls State was fascinating," she said. "It seemed that when (the politicians) stood up there and talked about their jobs and serving people, that it must be the finest thing anyone could possibly do."

Fascination bowed to reality when the teenaged Richards thought, "Girls don't go into politics."

Instead, Richards' interests turned to romance during her senior year when she started dating David Richards. After their first date, they attended every sports event and school dance together. The two were married in May 1953, right after graduation. Following a short honeymoon, David attended law school at the University of Texas, and Ann earned her teaching certificate. She taught for one year in an Austin junior high school.

Austin provided the political stimulation that Ann craved. She and David were active in the Young Democrats. They spent their Friday nights in lively debates with a group of like-minded political enthusiasts.

After he earned his law degree, David practiced law in Dallas, and the couple started their family. Between ironing shirts and caring for babies Ann still found time to be politically aware. Since she couldn't go out and join in the political activity, she brought the politics into her home by hosting Democratic functions. Their home became a revolving door, providing lodging for visiting activists and foreign dignitaries.

By the time her children started school, she was ready to get involved in local politics. She worked at the Kennedy/Johnson election headquarters in 1960, organized car shuttles to drive Democrats to the polls, distributed yard signs, and passed out bumper stickers.

In Dallas, Richards took a stand against racial discrimination by organizing the Dallas Committee for Peaceful Integration. In the struggle for fair pay for migrant workers, she boycotted Dallas grocery stores.

Richards' political experience was in demand when she moved back to Austin. She and her family had been in the area for two years when Sarah Weddington's campaign organizer called to see if Richards would help with Weddington's campaign image. The candidate went on to win a seat in the Texas House of Representatives.

Weddington later asked Richards to be her administrative assistant. Ann worked for Weddington one legislative session, gaining more insight into government. Some of her duties included planning legislative packages and dealing with constituents' problems.

Richards worked on campaigns in 1974 for Wilhelmina Delco and Gonzalo Barrientos. By 1975 Richards was ready to run another political campaign — her own.

When her husband, David, decided not to run for Travis County commissioner, the group asked Ann if she would run. She initially said no because she felt it would be impossible to be both a politician and a homemaker. David said, "Don't tell them no. You will wonder all your life whether you could have done it or not. And in the end, you'll probably be good at it."

Those proved to be prophetic words when public service did turn out to be Richards' strong point. Winning her first election, she served as Travis County commissioner for six years. Her charm and down-to-earth leadership style earned the respect and loyalty of her county workers. As commissioner, voter registration and human services were high on her list of program reforms.

But her success strained the couple's relationship, and eventually they would divorce.

During her 1988 campaign for state treasurer, one of her opponents called a press conference about Richards' past problems with alcohol. She had confronted her problem and was successful in her recovery.

Richards answered questions about the charges and corrected all misinformation. "I felt sort of sad about having to go through the whole process in public, but what was intended as a scandalous revelation was turned to my favor by the fact that I didn't run and hide from it."

Richards won the election, becoming the most successful treasurer in Texas history. For eight years she ran the best treasury in the nation. She updated collection procedures, cut many unnecessary regulations, and deposited the state's money in high-yield investments. Treasury investments earned $1.3 billion during Richards' first year in office.

It's hard to believe that the young girl who thought women couldn't run for political office would one day become the "billion-dollar treasurer," and, ultimately, governor of Texas.

Her divorce and her alcoholism made headlines during the heated gubernatorial race in 1991. Once more, she answered the charges with frank honesty. Her sincerity and remarkable public service record led to her victory over rancher Clayton Williams.

Richards shares the wisdom she has garnered along the way. She has spoken regularly at Girls State, telling the girls that today's women have more opportunities available to them than women of the past. Richards emphasizes that women "can have a good and wonderful life, but it only begins when they accept responsibility for it." Standing there before them, Ann Richards is living proof.

Chapter 7

They Excelled in Sports

Playing sports was as foreign to early Texas women as the moon was to sixteenth-century explorers. Sports were for men. In Greece, playing sports served as a religious tribute to Zeus. In Europe, sports served as a social diversion. To Native Americans, they were tests of strength.

For women in hoop skirts, bustles, and corsets, playing any sport was impossible. But then the Victorian ideal of the frail, swooning female gave way to the independent, active "flapper." Women forgot about corsets to enjoy the sports played by men.

By 1900, women had entered that most sacred shrine of sports, the Olympics. In 1914 they competed in floor exercises and had to wear long dresses. By 1920, women competed in swimming. They entered track and field events in 1928.

"Sports doesn't lead society; it reflects it," is the way Anita De Frantz, president of the Amateur Athletic Foundation of Los Angeles, explained sexism and racism in sports.

Before the civil rights movement the color barrier in sports had been broken by a few blacks: Jesse Owens in track, at the 1936 Olympics; Jackie Robinson in major league baseball in 1947; and Althea Gibson in tennis in 1950.

The feminist movement opened sports up to women. Physical education for girls became more challenging, with more than games and exercising. High school girls were competing in track and field events. In 1972, Congress outlawed sexual and racial discrimination to recipients of federal funds. In 1974, girls were admitted to Little League baseball.

Just as man has explored the moon, women have made sports history.

Mildred Didrikson Zaharias

A Woman Called Babe

Mildred Ella Didrikson was named the greatest woman athlete by the Associated Press and was woman athlete of the year six times. She was All-American basketball player for three years, often making thirty points a game. She held or tied the world record in four track and field events and won gold medals in the 80-meter hurdles and javelin and tied for first place in the high jump in the 1932 Olympics. In golf, she was the leading money-winner on the Ladies Professional Golf Association tour four years in a row. She was a woman called "Babe."

Babe was the nickname classmates gave to Mildred because they thought she played baseball like Babe Ruth. Mildred's sister, Lillie, said, "Babe was the best at everything."

Didrikson, born June 26, 1911, grew up in Beaumont, Texas. The Didrikson family's seven children were expected to do chores. Babe never let chores get in the way of her sports, though. Sent on an errand, she hurdled hedges. Scrubbing floors, she slid around the soapy floor on scrub brush skates.

Despite the interference of chores, Babe worked to become the greatest athlete that ever lived. She practiced running for the Olympics. She practiced basketball with the boys. Someone once asked Didrikson if there was anything she didn't play when she was a child. She replied, "Yeah, dolls."

To make money to support her training, Babe worked in a

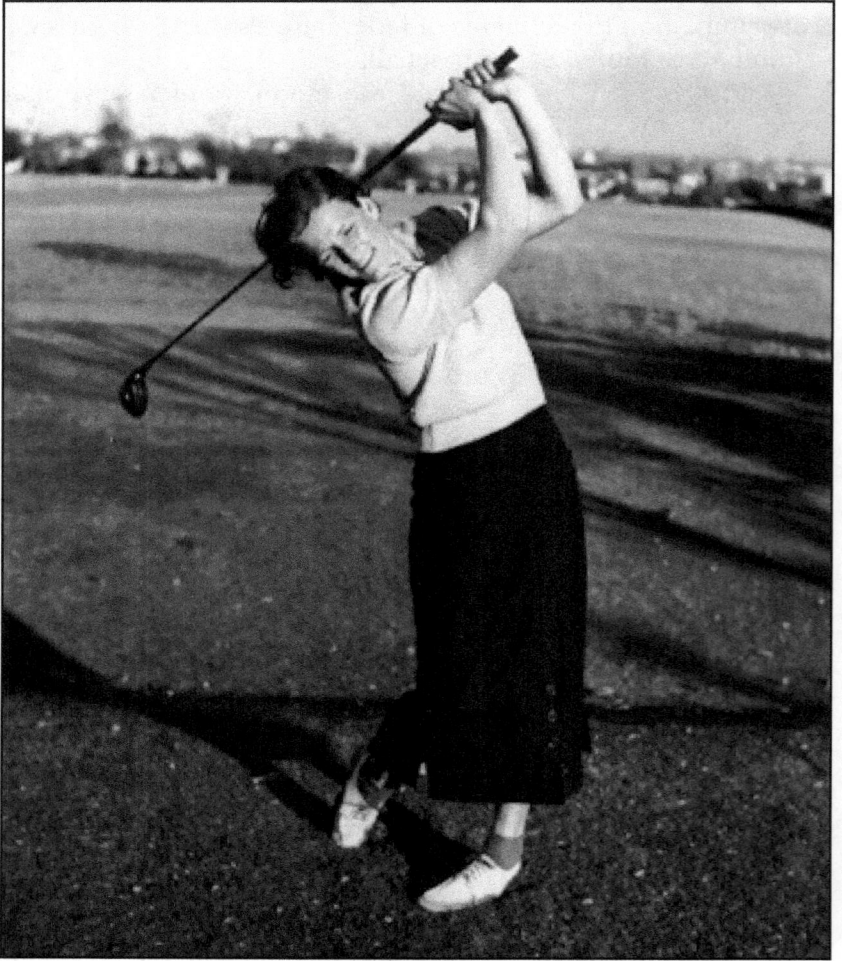

MILDRED DIDRIKSON was known worldwide as "Babe."
— Courtesy of University of Texas Institute of Texan Cultures

fig-packing plant for thirty cents an hour and sewed potato sacks for one cent each.

By the time she reached high school, Babe had excelled at all sports available to her. Basketball was her favorite. At seventeen she was on the all-city and the all-state basketball team.

At nineteen Babe moved to Dallas, where she worked for the Employer's Casualty Company and ran for the company-financed track team, the Golden Cyclones. In her first competition with the Cyclones, Babe entered four events and won them all. She got first place in three events, setting records by throwing the baseball 296 feet and running the eighty-meter hurdles in twelve seconds.

The team coach asked Babe to compete for the Cyclones again in 1932. She would be the only member on the team. There was no way the Golden Cyclones could win with only one entry — and a girl at that! Or so the other teams thought.

Babe threw the shot put thirty-nine feet, six and one-fourth inches for first place. She threw the javelin one hundred thirty-nine feet, three inches for first place. She threw the baseball two hundred seventy-two feet, two inches and won first place. She won first place in the eighty-meter hurdles and the broad jump. Then, slowing down, she tied for first place in the high jump and dropped to fourth in the discus. But she had won the track meet for the Cyclones and had qualified for five Olympic events.

At the 1932 Olympics in Los Angeles, Babe set records and won gold medals in the eighty-meter hurdles and the javelin.

In the high jump, Babe cleared the bar at five feet, five and one-fourth inches. So did Jean Shiley. The judges disqualified Babe because she had used the western roll style. She was later given a first place medal by the Olympic committee and named woman athlete of the year by the Associated Press.

Sports-conscious Americans followed the news and thrilled at the accomplishments of "The Babe." She was told, "You're making sports history. Girls everywhere are watching what you do."

In 1933 Babe took her family to California because she wanted to learn to play golf. Through golf, Babe finally found the sport she loved best. She practiced from five in the morning until midnight to perfect her golf game.

Lillie remembered Babe, with tape on her sore hands, saying she had to hit just a few more. "Oh, how that girl worked for the things she wanted," Lillie recalled.

By the fall of 1934, Babe was ready to enter the Fort Worth Invitational Golf Tournament, and in 1935 she won the Texas Amateur Golf Championship.

A golf club company paid her to put her name on a set of clubs and do demonstrations. She could hit five balls, driving the fifth before the first one had hit the ground. As a professional, Babe wasn't eligible to enter amateur competition under U.S. Golf Association rules.

In January 1938 Babe entered a professional tournament in Los Angeles. Her threesome included the wrestler George Zaharias, known as "the Weeping Greek from Cripple Creek." Zaharias, a good-natured giant of a man, remembered, "I put my arms around her in a wrestling hold for the photographers and said, 'You're mine, you know that.'" They were married on December 23, 1938, in St. Louis, Missouri.

Wanting to compete as an amateur again, Babe gave up professional competition for three years. After the U.S. Golf Association reinstated her amateur rank, Babe won the Western Women's Open Golf Tournament in 1946 and 1947 during a seventeen-match winning streak.

In 1947 Babe was one of ninety-nine women entering the British Women's Amateur Tournament. She had been told that "American women never win the tournament." That challenged Babe to win by five strokes, making her the first American woman to win the British Open. President Harry S. Truman sent her a telegram of congratulations for "representing the country well," and the mayor of Denver presented her with a key to the city.

In 1953, when Babe learned that she had cancer, she fought the disease with the same determination that she had fought opponents in sports. With her bag of golf clubs propped in the corner of her hospital room, her devoted husband by her side, and millions of fans sending messages of hope, Babe kept an optimistic outlook. She posed for newspaper photographs to encourage other cancer patients who might be cheered by her recovery.

In forty-three days she was out of the hospital. In one month she was practicing her golf swings. In two months she played nine holes with a friend.

In 1953 the Babe Zaharias Open was started in her honor in her hometown of Beaumont. The next year she won five U.S.

Women's Open tournaments and received the Associated Press Woman Athlete of the Year Award. She was honored by the American Cancer Society and was a guest of President Dwight Eisenhower at the White House.

By 1956 her old enemy, cancer, had attacked her body again, and it proved to be the only opponent to ever beat Babe. She died on September 27, 1956, at the age of forty-five.

Mildred Didrikson "opened the doors for girls and women in sports, . . . and gave people with cancer new hope and spirit." For that, we remember a woman called Babe.

BARBARA JACKET

She Coaches Winners

Runners pushed their toes against the starting blocks and took their stance. Barbara Jacket, head coach for the United States Women's Track Team in the 1992 Olympics, strained to see. The sun glowed white-hot in a hazy Barcelona sky.

The starter's gun cracked and runners sprang forward. A trickle of sweat rolled down Jacket's temple as she watched Evelyn Ashford rush up on Esther Jones and strain toward her in a two-handed pass in the lead leg of the race.

Jacket held her breath during the next two legs of the race. She let it out with a gasp as anchor Gwen Torrence sprinted ahead of the Unified Team's Irina Privalova for the gold. Jacket glanced skyward. The Barcelona sun beamed.

But Jacket couldn't relax with only a 100-meter relay win. There was still the 400 relay. "As the head coach, I wanted things to be perfect," she said.

Pushing athletes to perfection is common for Jacket. In 1976 she sent five of her Prairie View A&M track stars to the Olympics. She coached the women's track team to twenty national championships, twelve Indoor Southwest Athletic Conference Championships, and seven consecutive outdoor and cross-country titles.

In 1980 she was head coach of the Pacific Conference

BARBARA JACKET coached the 1992 Olympic track team.
— Courtesy of Public Information Office,
Prairie View A&M University

Games in Christ Church, New Zealand. In 1981 she was head manager of the World University Games in Bucarest, Romania. She was head coach of the National Sports Festival in Colorado Springs in 1983; University Games in Kobe, Japan, in 1985; and the World Championship in Rome in 1987.

In the 1992 Olympics, with a gold medal in the 100-yard relay and a silver medal in the 400-yard relay, Jacket's most exciting moment "was when we finished running the four-by-four hundred and it was all over."

The pressure began on November 27, 1989, when Jacket learned that she would be head coach of the Olympic staff for track and field. Coaches, picked according to their specialty, are chosen four years before the games by the Olympic Committee. Jacket, one of three women and the only black on the six-member staff, would be in charge of relay and sprints.

Jacket resigned as athletic director at Prairie View A&M, saying, "I didn't want to be divided. I didn't want either team to suffer."

After her resignation on June 21, 1991, Jacket turned her attention to the Olympics. After the staff had worked out problems, they met with the team. Jacket told the athletes, "We're going to do it this way. If you've got a problem you need to talk about it now."

She feels that the athletes' opinions are important to the focus of winning. "You don't try to change what got them there," said Jacket.

In 1991 the Olympic staff was responsible for the World University Games in Sheffield, England. They observed the Pan American Games in Cuba and the World Championship Games in Japan.

After the Olympic trials in June, the top three athletes and the relay team competed in France. On July 23, after moving into the Olympic Village in Barcelona, the relay team competed in Italy. "To get our timing down," Jacket explained.

By the time their events started on July 30, 1992, Jacket's pressure on herself was high. She said, "If they make a mistake, it's going to be me. If they do well, it's going to be them."

Jacket strives to get along well with her athletes. "If they like you, they'll perform. If they don't, they'll go right down the drain."

Born December 26, 1935, in Port Arthur, Texas, Jacket developed an early interest in sports.

"We were way before our time," said Jacket about the girls' athletics program at Lincoln School in Port Arthur. Her coach, Mrs. A. P. Guidry, had track teams for girls at a time when most schools didn't offer competitive sports for girls.

Sports was a year-round activity with Jacket. During football season she was a flag bearer with the band. Then she played basketball, followed by track. She went to the state track meet one year and threw baseball, shot-put, and discus. In the summer Jacket played softball on the city league.

In 1952 Jacket visited Tuskegee Institute in Alabama and decided to go there. As a single mother with three children, Eva Mae Getwood could not provide tuition for her daughter, Barbara.

"I'll get a job," Jacket told her mother. All summer Jacket left the house early every morning and returned home exhausted. She didn't have the nerve to tell her mother that she spent every day at the gym, playing basketball with the boys.

Her summer of practice at the boy's full-court game helped Jacket make the starting basketball team at Tuskegee.

At Tuskegee, Jacket majored in physical education, minored in biology, and spent the rest of her time practicing sports. In 1956 she went to the Olympic trials in Washington, D.C., where she tried out for shot-put and discus. She didn't make the team.

After graduation in 1958, Jacket taught physical education and coached basketball in Eufaula, Alabama. She competed in amateur track until 1959. "I was sitting under a tree, watching the other women on the team, and not feeling nervous about the events. I knew it was time to retire," Jacket said.

As a coach, Jacket looks for that nervousness in winning athletes. She said, "As long as you want to be a winner, you're going to have to be bothered. . . . If the adrenaline doesn't start, then it's time to retire."

In 1959 Jacket went back to Port Arthur to help care for her ill mother. She got a job as assistant basketball and track coach at Lincoln School.

After her forty-four-year-old mother died, Jacket started work on her master's degree at Prairie View A&M. In 1968 she became a professor in the Department of Health and Human Performance there. During her years at Prairie View, Jacket's coaching has brought achievement to the track team, the college, and herself.

The track team was named National Association of Intercollegiate Athletes National Outdoor Track and Field Champions in the Women's Division in 1985. They won first place at the championships in 1984, 1985, and 1986.

In appreciation of her contribution to women's track and field, Jacket received the Joseph J. Robichaux Memorial Award on December 12, 1992. On May 11, 1993, Jacket was inducted into the National Association of Intercollegiate Athletes Hall of Fame for her outstanding achievement as a coach of track and field. On October 16, 1993, Jacket's hometown declared a "Barbara Jacket Day" and dedicated Barbara Jacket Park. Port Arthur mayor Mary Ellen Summerlin said, "Barbara Jacket has brought honor, acclaim, and credit to Port Arthur . . . by setting an example for children to follow."

As athletic director, Jacket is among a very small group of women coaches in college. She admits that it's difficult for women in coaching. "A woman coach is competing in a man's world. It's almost like being black. You have to prove yourself over and over and over," she said.

Jacket has proved herself as a coach. Would she want to be an Olympic coach again? "No!" said Jacket, "I don't ever want to put that kind of pressure on myself again."

Chapter 8

They Became Scientists

From early times, women nursed the sick using home remedies passed down for generations. Native Texas women gathered wild plants as healing potions for the maladies of their time. They often shared their knowledge with the immigrants to their land.

One of those immigrants was "Grandma" Parker, who moved to Tokeen, Texas, in the early 1870s. Whether she gained her knowledge of medicinal plants from the Indians or from other sources, Parker successfully doctored the sick, using wild herbs she gathered from the area.

Like Parker, most pioneer Texas women practiced a form of folk-healing that was a blend of what they brought from the old country and what they learned in the new. They poulticed and plastered their "younguns'" croup. They soaked and salved their "oldsters'" aches. Standing beside the country doctor during home surgery or childbirth, they administered anesthetics with a drip of ether.

Standing at the wood stove, they stirred "burned flour" for the dysentery of a calf or child and sat up all night with their patient in a drafty cow-shed or equally drafty lean-to bedroom.

Early Texas women served as nurses, doctors, and undertakers, readying the dead for burial. Although they accepted their role as caregiver, few of them ventured into a man's place of medicine as doctors. But a few did, stripping off their aprons as homemakers/nurses and donning the white coats that marked them as professional doctors.

In time, as the study of healing grew to encompass mental and even social ills, women moved into those new fields as well.

MAY OWEN

Dr. May's Children

It was postmarked "Boston, 1917." May Owen opened the letter and read, "Although your grades are high, you have no outside interests. We deny your acceptance to nursing school."

Twenty-six-year-old Owen was disappointed, but she had learned long ago to hide her feelings. Born in Falls County on May 3, 1891, the sixth of eight children, she had suppressed her grief when her mother died. Accepting her role of farm hand as her father eked out a substandard living, she hid her desire for material wealth.

Reading the letter again, Owen sighed. "I didn't want to be a nurse, anyway," she said, like the fox about the out-of-reach grapes. But Owen's out-of-reach goal was really to be a doctor, a dream that began when she was nine years old.

She first thought of becoming a veterinarian because she liked taking care of animals on her father's farm. Once she saved a cow and calf during a difficult delivery. She was disappointed when the veterinarian told her, "Being a vet is a man's job."

When she saw the country doctor, who came by horseback to care for her dying mother, Owen decided that she would become a doctor.

When she told her father that she wanted to become a doctor, he replied, "Get this silly idea out of your head right now. Your place is here on the farm."

Owen didn't put the idea out of her head. Instead, she studied to learn everything she could. When she graduated from sev-

DR. MAY OWEN fulfilled her dream to attend medical school and later helped others do the same.
— Courtesy of Dr. Charles Rush

enth grade, she had the highest grades in the class. Since there was no high school nearby, Owen's education seemed to be over. She had been out of school for eight years when her older brother, who was working in New Mexico, sent money for her to attend high school in Fort Worth.

Her education would continue. Owen helped with expenses by working as an assistant teacher and later in Terrell's medical laboratory in downtown Fort Worth.

May gave her full energy to whatever job she did. She knew how to work hard from her years on the farm. Her hands were scarred from years of cotton picking. Her back was strong from years of carrying water pails and firewood.

She continued to dream of medical school and sent off applications. Receiving only rejections from medical schools, she finally accepted a job to teach after graduation from Texas Christian University in 1917. Then she was accepted at Louisville Medical College.

Owen told her father that she would be going back to school in the fall. He asked, "Aren't you educated enough?"

When she told him that she was going to medical school, he said, "I still can't understand why."

Others who couldn't understand why a woman was going to medical school were her fellow classmates, all males, at Louisville Medical College. Owen didn't know that they had petitioned the dean to have her removed from classes. She knew only that they welcomed her like the return of the plague from the Middle Ages.

But Owen soon won the trust and friendship of her classmates. She explained her cure for her own particular plague of prejudice against her as a woman by saying, "I've tried to stay in a woman's place, and I think that's helped me more than anything else." The men showed their acceptance of May by taking her to Derby races and out to eat.

During the flu epidemic of 1918, Owen realized that there was just so much that medicine could do if the cause of a disease was unknown. Deciding to study pathology as her medical specialty, May said, "I knew that to be a competent and good pathologist I would have to bury myself in my work." She thanked God that she had an insatiable intellectual curiosity and that she had conditioned herself to get by on small amounts of sleep and food.

After graduation from medical school in 1921, Dr. Owen returned to Terrell Labs. To Dr. Owen, being a pathologist was like being a medical detective. Hunched over her microscope, she found clues in the tissue she studied. Using those clues like pieces in a jigsaw puzzle, Dr. Owen had the whole picture and the answer to medical problems.

One example of Dr. Owen's detective work was in 1931, when she traced an epidemic of sheep deaths to the company that produced the molasses-laced pellets they were fed. Lubricating oil from machinery used in making the pellets was poisoning the sheep.

In February of 1935 Dr. Owen solved another medical mystery. She found that the talc in the glove powder used by surgeons caused the growth of nodules in their patients. Dr. Owen presented her findings to the Texas State Medical Association. Powder manufacturers replaced the talc with a nontoxic ingredient. On May 27, 1936, the Texas State Pathological Society awarded Dr. Owen a Certificate of Meritorious Research.

Pathology was Dr. Owen's first love, and education was second. In 1946 she helped four veterans who were going to school on the GI Bill. Those four young men were the first of many who received Dr. Owen's help. She loaned money interest-free and spoke in their behalf with school administrators. She referred to them as her "boys and girls," feeling as much pride in them as if she were their mother.

"This is my way of thanking all the people who helped me get my education . . . and I hope those I help will give someone down the line a boost," she said.

She also spent her time, energy, and money to help establish institutions of learning. She planned and worked almost twenty years for a museum because she felt that it would ". . . educate the public about health and medicine." On September 14, 1963, she took part in the dedication ceremonies for the Dr. May Owen Hall of Medical Science at the Fort Worth Museum.

In 1965 she saw the completion of another project she had helped with, Tarrant County Junior College. She was elected to the board of trustees for the college. In 1974 she donated money to establish a department for the study of pathology at Texas Tech University.

One day Dr. Owen found a long-forgotten letter filed away in her papers. The postmark was Boston, 1917. Dr. Owen remembered her anguish at being rejected by the nursing school so long ago.

But that rejection had turned out to be a blessing for May Owen and for mankind. One of those first medical students who was helped by Dr. Owen summed up that blessing in Dr. Owen's eulogy after her death in 1988. Dr. Charles A. Rush said, ". . . how many untold thousands have benefited from her practice of medicine which spanned more than sixty years? How many have been affected by the discoveries she made throughout her career? How many millions have been ministered to by the physicians whom she inspired through her leadership and activity in the Texas Medical Association?"

SARAH WILLIAMS

A Better World

In 1859, Charles Joe Robinson, a free black, was born in Mississippi. He knew black slaves. He survived the Civil War. He was part of the social revolution called Reconstruction. He moved to Texas, graduated from Prairie View A&M College, and became a teacher. He dreamed of a better world.

In 1880, James Robinson was born in Texas. He knew poor black laborers who lived in fear of the Ku Klux Klan. He lived with segregation — with being turned away from restaurants and hotels. He and his wife were teachers. He hoped for a better world.

In 1949, Sarah Robinson was born to James and his wife in Houston, Texas. She watched the freedom rallies. She saw the passage of laws ending segregation. Eventually she graduated from the University of Texas in Austin and became a sociology professor at Prairie View A&M. She now sees the rise of crime and drug use and knows that we must continue to work toward a better world.

Sociology professor SARAH WILLIAMS contributes time and expertise to help make society better.
— Courtesy of Public Information Office, Prairie View A&M University

Sarah Robinson Williams is proud of the examples set by her grandfather and father as leaders in the black community of their time. She admired her adoptive mother, Lizzie Robinson, who taught poor women in the community about cleanliness and nutrition.

In Columbus, Texas, Williams had a comfortable life because her father owned three funeral homes and rental properties by the time he retired from teaching. But her social life was restricted to her own neighborhood. Williams remembers that the only whites she saw in her neighborhood were women driving big cars. She watched her neighbors, dressed in starched maid uniforms, slide into the back seat for the trip across town.

Williams felt anticipation as she left that neighborhood at the age of thirteen to attend boarding school in San Antonio, Texas. There were white teachers and Hispanics in addition to the black students. Besides being free to shop and go to movies in downtown San Antonio, Williams had the opportunity for a better education than the state-provided one for minority students.

After her graduation from the St. Peter Claver Academy in 1965, Williams attended the University of Texas at Austin. When she graduated in 1970 with a bachelor of science degree, Williams followed Lizzie Robinson's example and became a social case worker. She earned her master's degree in social work at the University of Houston in 1972 and started teaching at Prairie View A&M.

At the first faculty/staff meeting on October 3, 1972, she was so impressed by Robert Williams, an industrial technician at the college, that she said, "That's the man I'm going to marry."

And she did, on her birthday, December 27, 1975. They have a son and a daughter and live in Prairie View, where Mr. Williams now has his own construction company.

Williams earned her doctorate degree in philosophy at the University of Texas in 1978. As a sociology professor, Williams takes a professional look at the change of attitudes on college campuses. The era of protest marches gave way to the era of fun and noncommitment. The selfish "Me-generation" turned into the serious "World-Conscious" generation. "Students today worry more about jobs and feel more stress to do well in college," Williams said.

Williams sees that same stress affecting families. "Family life is suffering from the hurried life of everybody working," she explained. Williams feels that families are under stress due to tight money and less free time together.

That stress and breakdown of family life is affecting the children, according to Williams. Her advice to parents is, "Be involved with your children. Spend time together doing nothing." Williams sees children stressed out by too many scheduled activities.

"Nothing takes the place of parents," Williams said about the importance of being together as a family. As a licensed marriage counselor, Williams tries to help couples stay together. She feels that for the sake of the children couples should avoid divorce.

Williams sees lack of parental influence as the major cause of problems among young people today. With both parents working, children are on their own more. "But sometimes they sneak out even if their parents are home, and, often, they are allowed to go out," she said. "The parents just don't realize they're getting into trouble," she added. Williams feels that curfew laws would prevent crimes by kids by keeping them off the street late at night.

"Gangs are a substitute for belonging to something positive," according to Williams. "With strong families there's less chance of joining a gang." She sees an ever-growing tie between gang membership and drug use.

At the Chappell Hill Drug Rehabilitation Center, Williams trains drug counselors. She teaches counselors to define the problem or reason for drug use and set goals to eliminate the use. Counselors must establish rapport with the person they are helping and follow up with needed support to continue that help.

Williams was invited to attend a seminar at Boston University sponsored by the National Endowment for Humanities. She plans to use the information from the seminar entitled "Morality and Society" with her classes in sociology, as a certified social worker, and as a volunteer for the Harris County Hospital District. It will also be helpful in her work on the National Steering Committee of the Young Women's Christian Association.

In Prairie View, Williams volunteers for church activities and with the local group of Jack and Jill of America, a nationwide service organization for young adults.

Williams has served for six years on the advisory board of the

Chapel Speakers group at Prairie View A&M. The advisory board brings outstanding community leaders as speakers to present positive role models and social awareness to the students. In May of 1994, Williams received the Chapel Award as board chairman. Williams feels that the Chapel Speakers give the students incentive to become better citizens in the world they are about to enter as leaders of tomorrow.

Williams sees a world of better race relations in some places, but she is concerned about the existence of hate groups. She hears the troublemakers speak against blacks, Jews, and Asians. Williams asks, "Do students have the right to speak against minorities? Do minority students have rights?" as she works to help people live together in a better world.

Chapter 9

They Preserved the Law

The western United States was wild and lawless in the 1800s. Gunfighters, thieves, and Mexican bandits took what they wanted regardless of who had to die.

Texas was custom-made for the lawless. Miles of frontier bordered Mexico, a short jump across the Rio Grande. Between the Rio Grande and Pecos rivers, desperadoes could find a hiding place in the rugged mountain range. The Gulf of Mexico stretched along the eastern coast with pirates, like the legendary Jean Lafitte, navigating the waters around Buffalo Bayou and Galveston Bay as early as 1817.

Criminals moved into the new territory along with settlers. By 1821 the state's founding father, Stephen F. Austin, had hired hardy frontiersmen to ride the ranges. They caught cattle rustlers, stopped Indian raids, handled brawling settlers, and fought gunfighters. By the mid-1800s those lawmen, called Rangers, were facing cold-blooded outlaws like John Wesley Hardin and Black Jack Ketchum.

The Rangers, whose techniques were not always by the book in their early years, could be heavy handed. They often shot first and asked questions later.

Texas women had their part in breaking the law. Belle Starr, caught up in the post-Civil War turmoil against Carpetbaggers, provided refuge to outlaws. If Starr was Dallas' "Bandit Queen" of the 1800s, then Bonnie Parker was its gangster moll of the 1900s. When gangster Clyde Barrow walked into the Dallas cafe where she was a waitress, it didn't take Bonnie long to ditch her apron for a Tommy gun.

But most Texas women chose the right side of the law, protecting their children and homes from attack of all kinds. Later, as they took their place beside men, they served as police officers, lawyers, and judges in a more civilized state.

Sarah Tilghman Hughes

Swearing in a President

At 11:40 on the morning of November 22, 1963, Federal District Judge Sarah Tilghman Hughes watched television coverage of President John F. Kennedy's arrival in Dallas. On the screen the president smiled and squinted in the glare of sunlight as he shook hands with the people pressed against the fence. They waved signs lettered, "Welcome JFK." The first lady, in a pink wool suit, reached for the bouquet of roses held toward her by a little girl.

Judge Hughes remembered the sense of dread she felt when she learned that Kennedy would visit Dallas on his tour. She agreed with those who said, "Dallas is not a favorable climate for the president."

At the Trade Mart, where thousands gathered to hear Kennedy speak that day, Judge Hughes noted that the president was late. At 12:50 it was announced, "The president's been shot!"

Hughes, like many others, decided to go home. As she maneuvered her car through the Dallas traffic, police across town chased a suspect, and the president lay in Parkland Memorial Hospital, mortally wounded.

At Parkland, the car carrying Vice-president Lyndon B. Johnson glided close to the curb. Secret Service agents tried to

JUDGE SARAH HUGHES administered the presidential oath to Lyndon Johnson amidst tragedy in 1963.
— Courtesy of University of Texas Institute of Texan Cultures

cover the bulk of the large man in a western-cut suit. They almost carried his petite wife, "Lady Bird," in their rush to get them to safety in the hospital. Inside, the vice-president paced the small room like a caged tiger.

At 1:00 P.M. he was told, "The president's dead." He was also told, "Nobody knows if the shooting was done by one man or if it's a conspiracy to overthrow the government." Johnson had to get back to Washington as soon as possible, but he would be sworn in as president before he left Dallas. The attorney general suggested that Sarah Hughes administer the oath of office.

Johnson had lobbied for Sarah Hughes in 1961 when President Kennedy appointed her as federal judge. Those who opposed the appointment said that, at sixty-five, Hughes was too old, and, as a woman, she was not qualified.

Hughes had been proving her qualifications since her arrival in Texas in 1922.

Born in Baltimore, Maryland, on August 2, 1896, Hughes grew up with a zest for life. In high school and college she played basketball, worked on the campus newspaper, and participated in Delta Gamma sorority. After she graduated from Western High School in 1913 and Goucher College in 1917, Hughes taught at Salem Academy and College in Winston-Salem, North Carolina.

In 1919, Hughes enrolled at George Washington Law School and worked with the Washington, D.C. Police Department.

In law school Hughes was again active in extracurricular activities, including student politics. She served in the law school senate with her future husband, George Hughes, of Texas. They were married on March 13, 1922, and moved to Dallas, where they practiced law together.

In Texas, Hughes found that law was practiced by men in striped suits pleading the case of defendants brought to justice by lawmen wearing silver badges before an all-male jury with a man in judicial robes presiding. Women had no voice in Texas law.

Elected to the Texas Senate in 1930, Hughes worked to give Texas women more rights as citizens. She introduced a bill to give married women legal rights equal to those of men and single women. She worked on a bill to give women the right to serve on juries, but it didn't pass until 1954. In 1935, after her appointment by Governor Allred as a state district judge, Hughes was reelected four more times.

In 1952 she was nominated as a vice-presidential candidate at the Democratic National Convention because of her efforts to get equal rights for women.

Working to give women equal rights was always a top priority with Judge Hughes. She said, "Laws alone are not enough. They have to be carried out. Attitudes must be changed. Each woman must set her goal and then strive to reach it."

Judge Hughes had always followed that advice whether on the bench or as president of the National Federation of Business and Professional Women. The five-foot, one-inch Hughes had never been intimidated by anyone. She accepted the challenges.

On November 22, 1963, she accepted another challenge. She heard newsman Walter Cronkite announce to the nation, "The president is dead."

At Love Field the convoy of cars halted. Jacqueline Kennedy, her pink suit spattered with her husband's blood, followed his casket onto the plane.

"We've got to take off immediately!"

"Not until Johnson has taken the oath of office!"

"Is Judge Hughes here?"

"She's on her way."

Sarah Hughes maneuvered her car past the Spirit of Flight statue at Love Field. Two men rushed to meet her. As they escorted her onto the plane, one thrust a card into her hand and said, "Here's the oath." Someone handed her a Bible.

Judge Hughes glanced at the tense faces of the staff members gathered for the oath. They looked like pawns waiting to be put into play for a new game. Johnson towered above them like the king. His first lady was at his right side, and Mrs. Kennedy stood regally on his left. Judge Hughes took her place facing President Johnson.

Each person in the room seemed deep in his own thoughts. No one moved except the photographer.

Judge Hughes' voice quavered as she began, "I do solemnly swear that I will —"

Johnson laid his large hand across Kennedy's personal Bible, covering the initials, JFK, and echoed the judge's words to the end: ". . . and defend the Constitution of the United States."

96

The jet engines roared into life. It was 2:38 P.M.

Standing by her car, Hughes watched the plane taxi down the runway. A placard, with the words "Welcome JFK" on it, fluttered briefly in the wind from the jet engines before settling into the mud at her feet.

Hughes knew that being the first woman to swear in a president would bring her fleeting fame, but she was more interested in doing her job to bring justice and improvement. She presided over the Sharpstown case which brought scandal to a number of Texas politicians. She ruled in favor of defendants in discrimination cases. She took on the challenge of improving the Dallas County Jail, which she called "a factory for crime." She gave speeches and wrote articles for the continued equal rights of women in the Western Hemisphere. She believed in rehabilitation over punishment for juvenile offenders.

Sarah Hughes set an example for others by meeting the challenges in her life. She would continue to meet the challenges until her death on April 25, 1985.

MARRIE REYNOLDS GARCIA

Don't Call Her a Rangerette

Hollywood came calling, offering Marrie Reynolds Garcia a movie deal. Her life story is a hot commodity. It seems everyone in the media throughout Texas wants to broadcast her accomplishment over the airways and splash her story across their front pages.

As proud as Garcia is of achieving her dream, she does not want to exploit her position. She will not tarnish the reputation of the 170-year-old organization she has worked for years to join.

Garcia made history by earning an appointment to the Texas Rangers. She was one of the first women to pass the Ranger examination, qualifying her for appointment to the elite law enforcement agency.

According to Garcia, "Being the first woman didn't have

MARRIE GARCIA wears the badge of the state's legendary lawmen, the Texas Rangers.
— Courtesy of Marrie Reynolds Garcia

anything to do with my decision to become a Ranger. I'm still proud to be the first one, but I don't go around telling everyone."

In fact, Garcia postponed taking the Ranger examination for a year, hoping that another woman would pass the test and spare her the notoriety of being the first female Ranger. "I didn't want to be in the spotlight with all the media attention," she admitted.

After promotions were made in August of 1993, Garcia received phone calls from television stations, newspapers, and movie producers. When Garcia reported to her duty station in Garland, Texas, she was resolute in her decision not to talk to the media. Reporters had to settle for press releases from the Texas Rangers' public affairs office in Austin.

Garcia felt it was important to remain low key about her historic achievement if she wanted to fit in with fellow Rangers. "The guys were nervous," Garcia recalled. "They thought we (women) were going to be showboats with all the newspapers and television stations. I can understand that they would be worried about changes after things being one way for so long."

Texas Rangers' history was interwoven with the state's history when Stephen F. Austin organized the law enforcement group. The earliest account of Ranger history is found in a letter written by Austin in 1821. He described the group he founded as Rangers employed to protect settlers. Out of necessity, the original Ranger had to be a fighting man who could outride, outshoot, and outfox the fierce Comanche warriors and, later, Mexican bandits who roamed the Texas frontier. Ranger history is rich with stories of courage and resourcefulness as these men squelched raids, cattle rustling, and the occasional rowdy settler.

Ranger captains L. H. McNelly and John Armstrong earned a place in history by subduing their era's notorious criminals — Mexican cattle thief Juan Cortina and Texas gunman John Wesley Hardin. In another era, Ranger Frank Hamer was coaxed out of retirement to track down the duo of Clyde Barrow and Bonnie Parker. The gangsters robbed banks and stores, killing over a dozen citizens and lawmen, in a path of terror that led from the Midwest to Louisiana.

Garcia had always admired the Texas Rangers. "It's prestigious. Not everyone can be a Ranger," she said. Garcia explained the requirements for becoming a Texas Ranger. Prospective agents need at least eight years of law enforcement experience. Four years of that experience must be with the Texas Department of Public Safety (DPS). Those who pass the required examination are interviewed by a review board with an overall score determined by combining the test and interview results. There were 208 DPS troopers who took the test with Garcia. Scorers in the top forty were interviewed and "appointed in the order of their ranking on the promotion list," according to the Texas Rangers' publicity office. In 1993 there were seven available duty assignments for the ninety-six-member agency. The state is divided into six Ranger companies.

Garcia's quest to join the Texas Rangers began over twenty years ago at Del Mar College in Corpus Christi. The Austin native planned to study physical education at Del Mar, but she soon discovered that police work interested her.

She earned a certificate and taught driver's education classes during the day. At night she attended college classes to earn sixty credit hours so she could enter the DPS Academy to become a state trooper. Garcia attended the grueling twenty-two-week-long academy in Austin.

Every morning Garcia and fellow cadets were up before dawn for physical training. The class' five women received the same training the 128 men received. In addition to running and push-ups, the cadets learned self-defense, including boxing. "About the second week I wondered, what am I doing? It's like boot camp, only worse," Garcia recalled.

Her training was more than physical, though. Each day the cadets spent hours learning state laws, safety, and DPS procedures. There was training in high-speed pursuit and other driving techniques. Cadets were trained to use a variety of firearms and practiced daily at the range. "The academy is stressful," Garcia said, "but it's necessary to find out what kind of stuff you're made of."

Following graduation from the academy, Garcia headed back to Corpus Christi for her first DPS assignment. She earned promotions over the years as she took tests and moved from station to station, working in Harlingen and San Antonio DPS units. She earned her sergeant's stripes during her ninth year as a DPS trooper while she was supervisor of the driver's license division.

She decided to take the Ranger's examination because investigative work appealed to her.

Today's Texas Rangers provide investigative assistance to police and sheriff's departments in Texas counties. Garcia said that smaller counties may not have the resources needed to investigate murders, missing person reports, and other serious crimes. "Anything we can do to help the officers in our counties we do," she said. "We may have better equipment . . . . We also provide our crime lab in Austin if they want to send evidence there."

Rangers work in cooperation with federal agencies such as the Federal Bureau of Investigation or the Drug Enforcement Agency if the cases involve a federal suspect. "The more people you have working on a crime, the better chance you have of catching the guy," Garcia said. She listed murder, theft, burglary, kidnapping, and gambling as examples of cases she has handled.

Garcia attended special schools to learn procedures and investigative techniques she would need to know as a Texas Ranger. New Ranger School provided the basics she would need for handling paperwork and advanced techniques in her new position.

Garcia, who always admired the Rangers, said she is amazed when she sees that the criminal suspects have their own admiration for the legendary Texas lawmen. "Sometimes people who won't talk to another investigator will spill their guts for the Rangers when they question them," Garcia said.

She says becoming a Texas Ranger was the culmination of years of planning and preparation. Now that she has achieved her goal, Garcia plans to spend the rest of her law career as a Ranger. Her practical advice to anyone who wants to reach a goal is: "If there's something that you really want to do, there may be sacrifices you have to make and they may not be pleasant, but it's worth it."

One sacrifice that Garcia has made is that she and her husband of eight years had to live in different cities when she was sent to Garland and her husband, Robert Garcia, a police officer with the city, stayed in San Antonio. Garcia said it was hard on them, but she counts herself lucky to have a husband who was on her side, supporting her dream. A year later she was transferred to the Ranger station in San Antonio.

101

Although it took over a century and a half before the Texas Rangers' barrier against women came down, Garcia does not blame the slow progress on the organization. She believes there are some practical reasons. For example, few women have the number of years' experience required to qualify to apply. Garcia also chuckles about the Rangers' uniform scaring away the more fashion-conscious woman.

Texas Rangers wear dress slacks or blue jeans with a western-cut shirt. Every Ranger straps on two belts, known as a double rig. One is a regular belt, while the other is a gun belt with holster.

"We wear boots and a cowboy hat," Garcia said. "In the summer we wear straw, and then change to a white felt hat in the winter."

Ranger badges are still stamped out of silver Mexican coins. Turn the badge over and you can see the design of the cinco peso.

History and tradition are as much a part of the Rangers' makeup as the boots or jeans, and Garcia wouldn't want it any other way. For her, as well as many Texans, the Rangers will always be the good guys in the white hats.

As for the Rangers who openly oppose women joining their domain, Garcia remains charitable. "Some men may have felt that since women haven't been allowed in, why do it now?" she said. "That's their opinion, but the guys I work with treat me like one of them. I get the same work and the same cases." Garcia shrugged her shoulders. "Other than getting the door opened for me, I'm treated just like one of the guys."

Chapter 10

They Keep Their Heritage Alive

Along the Rio Grande the Lipan Apache women, wearing clam shell jewelry, watched from their crude tents as Spaniards hacked through the thick palmetto growth. The native Texans greeted this new tribe of silver-helmeted, red-bearded men in friendship and traded with them. Indian women, taken captive by either the Spaniards or other tribes, often guided the explorers across the unmapped land of the Tejas Indians.

After the explorers came the Spanish colonists, who claimed the land and named the Indians as Spanish subjects. Along with Christianity, they brought the Indians serfdom and disease. The Native Americans resisted the white man's religion and the white man's rules, but they could not resist the white man's diseases.

Along the coast, Karankawa women fished in the Gulf and wove baskets from reeds. At Bolivar they saw the white man's fort, where cannons fired when they approached. They watched a woman named Jane Long fish in the Gulf waters. Left alone at the fort, she gave birth to a child there. When her husband was killed, Jane Long joined Stephen F. Austin's colony.

Austin and his aggressive Anglo-American colonists had settled on the Central Plains. They plowed the hunting grounds into fields, pushing the Indians from their plains. Those who didn't migrate south to Mexico died in smallpox epidemics.

French colonists couldn't keep their tenuous hold upon the pine thickets of East Texas. But other immigrants to the region, the Mound Dwellers from Alabama, adapted to the forest life. They learned to build log cabins like the white man's. They made friends with Texas' leader Sam Houston, and they survived. Even today, the strong women of that tribe work to keep their past alive and their future promising.

FRANCES BATTISE

Helping Her People

The Alabama Mound Dwellers survived in the Big Thicket of East Texas. Over the years they abandoned their mud structures built on mounds and cut the straight pine trees into logs for their houses. Now, conserving one of the few remaining native forests in the United States, the Alabama-Coushattas live in brick homes scattered among the tall pines of the Big Thicket.

Long ago, when their new corn crop matured, the tribe always put out their fires, which they thought possessed evil spirits that could destroy the crop. This ritual was called the Green Corn Ceremony. They had danced and chanted, asking for a good crop to feed their families through the coming year.

But when the missionaries came, they were told that the drums and the dances were pagan rituals. The Alabama-Coushattas silenced their drums and forgot their dances. They began to pray in the church of the missionaries. They lived like the white men and worshiped like them.

By the time Frances Battise was born, on April 22, 1941, there was no Green Corn Ceremony. The people on the reservation had forgotten the dances. They no longer crafted tools, wove baskets, or made pottery. They bought everything they needed in stores. The children went to the white men's schools and learned their ways.

"I don't like school," Battise had told her grandfather. "The

FRANCES BATTISE was the first woman elected to her tribe's ruling council.

teacher calls us 'Indian children' and makes us sit in the last row. The teacher thinks I'm dumb."

"You're not dumb," her grandfather responded. "The more you learn, the better your life will be. So you go to the white man's school and learn as much as you can."

Battise remembers that she was in seventh grade when she began to act on her grandfather's advice. "It was like a light suddenly came on," she said about her decision to do the best she could in school. She studied hard. Her grades improved, and she was honored as salutatorian of her graduating class at Big Sandy, Texas.

After graduation, she attended Lamar University School of Nursing, but she quit to get married. She went back to school to study nursing at Angelina College in Lufkin and passed her board exams to become a registered nurse in 1969. After returning to college in 1990, she earned her bachelor of science degree in 1993 and then began work toward her master's degree.

At the clinic on the Alabama-Coushatta reservation, Battise uses her health education degree to teach the people of her tribe how to care for themselves. Many people on the reservation have diabetes, and Battise hopes to teach them about diet, exercise, and medication to make their lives better. During the six years she has worked at the clinic, Battise has seen progress in fighting diabetes. A nutritionist, kidney specialist, pediatrician, and podiatrist make regular visits to the clinic. Patients who need hospital care are taken to Lufkin, Livingston, or Houston.

The clinic was named best in the area and was nominated for a national award. With pride, Battise and her staff accepted the award for the Alabama-Coushatta Health Clinic in September of 1994 in Nashville, Tennessee. The clinic was recognized for exemplary group performance by the Indian Health Service, part of public health services in the Department of Health, Education, and Human Services. Their "outstanding and specific contributions were recognized as providing a substantial improvement toward advancing the mission of the agency," according to Indian Health Service officials.

Battise, who was born in the hospital on the reservation, was raised by her grandparents. Her grandfather, Frank Walter Sylestine, was born in 1881, twenty-seven years after the land had been made into a reservation by the United States government. Battise's grandfather often told her, her two sisters, and her brother about the old ways. "We would sit on the porch and listen to his stories. That was before we had TV," Battise remembers.

In 1854, when the first 1,280-acre reservation was awarded to the Alabama-Coushatta tribes, it was divided into farms. "But the land was not very good for farming," Battise said, remembering the farm her grandfather had. Today each person on the reservation is given one acre but can ask for more land if they need it. On the 4,330-acre reservation today, where 478 tribe members live, there are very few farms.

Before farming, when the Alabama-Coushattas were hunters, the women had to solve the problems of the village and settle family disputes while the men were away. They grew strong and confident in making decisions and accepting a role of leadership. "The women always had a voice in the tribe," Battise said.

Battise has no trouble accepting her role as tribal leader. She has served on the tribal council since her election in 1980. In 1993, she was elected tribal chairperson, the first time a woman has held that position. Battise has been named one of 2,001 outstanding Indian women and is named in *Who's Who*.

As chairperson she presides at council meetings, where all business of the tribe is conducted in their native language. The tribal council, which is similar to a city council, oversees all tribal businesses, which include a restaurant, store, laundromat, campground, museum, and a radio station. There are also bus and train tours and dancing events on the reservation.

The main income for those on the reservation has been tourism since 1960. When the state saw that farming was not profitable, they agreed to fund a tourist complex. The state agency suggested that the Alabama-Coushattas perform native dances and sell handmade crafts. The problem was that they no longer danced or crafted on the reservation and had forgotten how.

But they have learned. Most of the dances they perform at the reservation are borrowed from other tribes. They no longer make pottery, but weave pine-needle baskets decorated with pine cones. The older people in the tribe have been important in teaching native crafts. Although some are in their seventies, they still work twenty hours a week. Battise feels that they are providing a valuable service to the tribe by teaching these skills to the young people.

Every year since the late 1960s, the Alabama-Coushattas have held a pow-wow during the first week of June. Many of the tribe members return for the homecoming and people from other tribes attend and take part in the dance contests. The highlights of the pow-wow is choosing a tribal princess. Entrants for the title are judged on their native costume and on their ability to tell a native folk tale. "Knowing their history helps build self-esteem in the younger people of the tribe," Battise said.

Battise and the tribe are working to preserve their heritage by improving the site where visitors can get a first-hand look at Native-American history.

River of Dreams

After the fall of the Alamo, most of Texas' men joined Sam Houston's army. They hoped to stop Santa Anna from driving the Anglo colonists from Texas.

Texas women gathered possessions and children to flee as refugees of war toward the east. According to T. R. Fehrenbach in his book *Lone Star,* "There were hundreds of tales of heroism and self-reliance, as the women struggled over the muddy roads toward the Sabine, without their men, abandoning their homes and the labor of years, with the smoke of the Mexican swath of destruction rising behind them."

When Sam Houston's army defeated Santa Anna at San Jacinto, Texas fulfilled her dream of independence and claimed land south to the banks of the Rio Grande. Zachary Taylor's troops patrolled the river in shallow draft riverboats.

With the riverboats came a new breed of men — their captains. Among the best of those captains was Richard King. He ran a shipping company with two other men, and during the Civil War they shipped cotton for southern farmers from Mexican ports to European markets.

When the Civil War had ended, and the last battle was

fought on the banks of the Rio Grande at Palmito Hill, King continued his steamboat shipping. Then the wide expanse of grasslands between Brownsville and Corpus Christi lured King. It was to that wild stretch of Texas that King took his young bride, Henrietta Chamberlain of Brownsville. They built a ranch house, raised their family, and started a ranching empire.

At King's death in 1885, that 500,000-acre empire was in debt. Henrietta got the ranch out of debt and built it into the modern King Ranch that it is today. The ranch has inspired many to keep up the ranching tradition — including a woman named Helen Groves.

HELEN GROVES

A Rancher Today

Helen Groves has had many close friends during her lifetime. She has known many of them from the day they were born. She has shared the highs and lows in her life with these friends as they worked side by side. Groves has learned a lot about life from them.

Her friends are not ordinary, though. They are the four-legged variety — horses. As far back as Groves can remember, horses have been part of her life.

"You have to get to know a horse to work with it," Groves said in a telephone interview from her Silverbrook Ranch near Baird, Texas. She has been training quarter horses most of her adult life.

Horse training is a full-time job. Not long after the foal is born, it learns to accept human contact. A few days after its birth, the trainer straps a halter on the foal to help the young horse grow accustomed to being led. After a year, the trainer saddles the horse for the first time, mounts, and rides short distances. Then the trainer can teach the horse to follow the rider's signals. After this basic knowledge is taught, the horse is ready to be trained for his sport.

Horses are trained for thoroughbred racing, barrel racing,

109

Rancher HELEN GROVES lives the cowgirl life.
She was raised on the immense King Ranch.
— Courtesy of Helen Groves

and rodeo events including steer wrestling, calf roping, and cutting cattle. Groves' registered quarter horses are trained for cutting. Cutting is a method used by cowboys to sort cattle from a herd. Quarter horses are used for this task because they are quick and agile. They are capable of handling the starts, stops, and turns needed to guide a stray cow back to the herd or to separate cattle for branding.

Groves was born in San Antonio, Texas, but spent most of her childhood on the King Ranch. Her father worked as general manager of the vast spread located five miles west of Kingsville. Groves loved ranch life. The wide open spaces and the animals saved her from boredom.

Life on the ranch was an adventure for young Groves. When they played cowboys and Indians, children on the King Ranch felt that they had stepped back in time to the days of Billy the Kid and Annie Oakley. Sometimes Groves would ride horses alone across the dusty ranch and watch a deep red South Texas sunset melt into the horizon. Buffalo grass and mesquite grew as far as the eye could see.

Groves spent many hours following horse trainer Max Hirsch around the barns, watching him work the King Ranch thoroughbreds. She marveled at the time and effort he spent working with the majestic steeds. He trained many prize-winning racehorses. The most famous was Assault, who won the Triple Crown in 1946.

There was no school close to the ranch, so Groves' mother taught her at home with the Calvert System of Home Schooling.

Helen Groves' idyllic childhood on the ranch ended when she was old enough to attend high school. Her parents decided to send her to Kingsville High School and later transferred her to St. Mary's Hall, a San Antonio girls' school. Neither school held her attention long. She missed the ranch's horses. When her parents told her about the Fox Croft School in Virginia, she was delighted to find a school with an equestrian program. The boarding school offered jumping classes and fox hunting.

Groves loved the early morning fox hunts on sturdy cutting horses. She wasn't as fond of horse shows, which involved exhibiting horses in their breed category. She liked the events that involved activity — jumping, racing, and hunting.

While she was a student at Fox Croft, she won a horse race on a quarter-mile track. Groves developed a deep admiration for quarter horses. That admiration prompted her to raise them on the first ranch she owned in Virginia.

During the early years of her marriage, Groves combined young motherhood with her love of horses. She worked with a pony club for girls, an international organization that teaches basic horsemanship. Lessons included how to care for the horses and equipment, how to ride, and how to compete in fox hunts and cattle round-ups.

Groves' six children developed their own love for horses. One daughter is part owner of a racehorse, while another daughter has a ranch in San Antonio. The other children ride in a variety of sporting events. Her son plays polo.

Today Groves puts in long days at Silverbrook Ranch, twenty-five miles east of Abilene, breeding and training quarter horses and thoroughbreds for sale. Hirsch, her old friend from the King Ranch days, still advises her on training techniques. "Some horses are smart, some are not so smart," Groves said. "They learn by repetition. I try not to take a second step in training until they learn the first."

Although she developed a back problem that caused her pain when she rode, Groves resumed horseback riding in 1972 despite her doctor's orders. She rides in cutting horse competitions in the United States as well as other countries. Groves even traveled to Australia for an international cutting horse contest. The American team of four riders had to borrow horses for the event. (Borrowing horses is a common practice in international competitions.) Every year the two countries take turns hosting the event sponsored by the National Cutting Horse Association.

A cutting horse competition demonstrates the team work necessary between horse and rider. The event reveals the training that allows a horse to select a calf and keep it from returning to the herd. The horse is trained to react to the calf's movement with very little direction from the rider.

Groves and her horse were high scorers for her team in Australia, although the team didn't win that year. But for Groves, any chance to work with horses gives her a winning feeling.

Bibliography

Chapter 1

Chipman, Donald E. *Spanish Texas*. Austin: University of Texas Press, 1992.

Connor, Seymour V. *Texas, A History*. Arlington Heights, IL: AHM Publishing Co., 1971.

Daughters of the Republic of Texas. *The Alamo Long Barrack Museum*. Dallas, TX: Taylor Publishing Company, 1986.

Fehrenbach, T. R. *Lone Star, A History of Texas and the Texans*. New York: Collier Books, Macmillan Publishing, 1980.

Kingston, Mike. *A Concise History of Texas*. Houston, TX: Gulf Publishing Co., 1988.

Martinez, Rolando. "DRT Tries to Block Honorary Marker for Alamo 'Savior.'" *San Antonio Express News,* 1994.

Pope, Dorothy Lee. *Rainbow Era on the Rio Grande*. Brownsville, TX: Springman King, 1971.

Ramirez, Alicia Hinojosa. *The Hinojosa Family from Mier, Tamp., Mexico to Texas*. Utica, KY: McDowell Pub., 1991.

Read, Phyllis J., and Bernard Witlieb. *The Book of Women's Firsts*. New York: Random House, 1992.

Rivard, Robert. "Remember the Alamo." *San Antonio Express News,* March 17, 1994.

Robinson, *C. M. Steamboats Once Traveled the River*. San Benito, TX: The *San Benito News,* November 1989.

Rybczyk, Mark Louis. *San Antonio Uncovered*. Plano, TX: Wordware Publishing, Inc., 1992.

Scott, Florence Johnson. *Royal Land Grants North of the Rio Grande*. Texian Press, 1969.

Turner, Martha Anne. *Clara Driscoll, a Painted Portrait*. Austin: Madrona Press, 1979.

Valley By-Liners. *Roots by the River*. Mission, TX: Border Kingdom Press, 1978.

Weatherford, Doris. *American Women's History*. New York: Prentiss Hall, 1994.

Chapter 2

Bush, Barbara. *A Memoir*. New York: Charles Scribner's Sons, 1994.

———. *Millie's Book*. New York: William Morrow and Company, Inc., 1990.

Chapter 3

Ash, Mary Kay. *Mary Kay*. New York, Harper & Row Pub., 1987.

Farnham, Alan. "Mary Kay's Lesson in Leadership," *Fortune,* September 20, 1993.

Kerr County Album. Kerr County Historical Commission, 1987.

Kerrville Daily Times. Wednesday, March 27, 1991.

Lasher, Patricia, and Beverly Bentley. *Texas Women: Interviews and Images*. Austin, TX: Shoal Creek Pub., 1980.

Valley By-Liners. *Rio Grande Roundup*. Mission, TX: Border Kingdom Press, 1980.

Chapter 4

Cowley, Malcolm. *Writers at Work*. New York: Viking Press, 1963.

Givner, Joan. *Katherine Anne Porter Conversations*. University Press of Mississippi 1987.

Hendricks, George, and Willene Hendricks. *Katherine Anne Porter*. Boston: G. K. Hall & Co., 1988.

Ivins, Molly. *Molly Ivins Can't Say That, Can She?* New York: Random House, Inc., 1992.

———. *Nothing' But Good Times Ahead*. New York: Random House, 1993.

Porter, Katherine. *The Collected Stories of Katherine Anne Porter*. New York: Harcourt, Brace, Jovanovich, 1969.

Rovin, Jeff. *Country Music Babylon*. New York: St. Martin's Paperbacks, 1993.

Tanner, James T. F. *The Texas Legacy of Katherine Anne Porter*. Texas Writer's Series #3. University of North Texas Press, 1990.

Chapter 5

Boyne, Walter J. *The Smithsonian Book of Flight*. Washington, DC: The Smithsonian, 1929.

Love, Dorothy M. *A Salute to Historic Black Women*. Chicago: Empak Publishing Company, 1984.

Rich, Doris L. *Queen Bess, Daredevil Aviator.* Washington, DC: Smithsonian Institution Press, 1993.

Rogers, Mary Beth, Sherry A. Smith, and Janelle D. Scott. *We Can Fly: Stories of Katherine Stinson and Other Gutsy Texas Women.* Austin: E. C. Temple: Texas Foundation for Women's Resources, 1983.

Smith, Jessie Carney. *Epic Lives.* Washington, DC: Visible Ink Press, 1993.

Verges, Marianne. *On Silver Wings.* New York: Ballantine Books, 1991.

Underwood, John W. *The Stinsons: The exciting chronical of a flying family and the 'planes that enhanced their fame.* Glendale, CA: Heritage Press, 1976.

Chapter 6

Angelo, B. *An Ethical Guru Monitors Morality. Time,* June 3, 1991.

"Announcing the 1994 Frontrunner Awards." *Newsweek,* December 5, 1994.

"Ann's Finest Moment." *Waco Tribune Herald,* June 5, 1995.

"Barbara Jordan." *Ebony,* October 10, 1972. Vol. 27.

Blue, Rose, and Corinne Naden. *Black American Achievements: Barbara Jordan.* Chelsea House Pub.

Brown, Chip. "Gov. Richards Defined Being a Texan." Associated Press, *Brownsville Herald,* November 12, 1994.

Haskins, James. *Barbara Jordan.* New York, Dial Press, 1977.

Jordan, Barbara (with Shelby Hearon). *Barbara Jordan, A Self-Portrait.*

Richards, Ann (with Peter Knobler). *Straight From the Heart.* New York: Simon and Schuster, 1989.

Solomon, Marva. "The Voices of Black Texans." *Texas Highways,* September 1993.

Chapter 7

Collins, David R. *Super Champ — The Story of Babe Didrikson Zaharias.* Austin, TX: Eakin Press, 1982.

Gustaitis, Joseph. "Babe Didrikson, America's Greatest Athlete." *American History Illustrated,* April 1987.

Lynn, Elizabeth A. *American Women of Achievement, Babe Didrikson Zaharias-Champion Athlete.* New York: Chelsea House, 1989.

Morse, Susan L. "Women and Sports." *Sports,* March 6, 1992.

Zaharias, Babe Didrikson. *This Life I've Led.* San Diego: A. S. Barnes & Co., 1955.

Chapter 8

Stafford, Ted. *May Owen, M.D.* Austin, TX: Eakin Press, 1990.

Chapter 9

Allread, Opal Howard. *Sarah T. Hughes Federal Judge: Case Study and Judges.* 1987.

Cobler, Sharon. "Women are Called 'Forgotten Majority.' " *Dallas Morning News,* December 19, 1975.

Davis, John L. *The Texas Rangers.* San Antonio: University of Texas Institute of Texan Cultures, 1991.

Dengus, Anne. *Book of Texas Lists.* Austin, TX: Texas Monthly Press, 1981.

Douglas, C. L. *The Gentlemen in the White Hats.* Austin, TX: State House Press, 1992.

Hughes, Judge Sarah T. "UN Commission Meets in Buenos Aires to Discuss Status of Women." *National Business Woman,* June 1960.

Report of the Warren Commission on the Assassination of President Kennedy. Introduction by Harrison E. Salisbury. New York: McGraw-Hill Book Company, 1963.

Chapter 10

Cantor, George. *North American Indian Landmarks.* Detroit, MI: Visible Ink Press, 1993.

Hunt, Dianna. "Tourism Gives Tribe a Boost." *Houston Chronicle,* June 26, 1994.

Warren, Betsy. *Indians Who Lived in Texas.* Dallas, TX: Steck-Vaughn, 1970.

Wooldridge, Ruby A., and Robert B. Vezzetti. *Brownsville, A Pictorial History.* Norfolk, VA: Donning Company Publishers, 1982.